D1766970

Bake
with
Maw Broon

EAT, DRINK
& BE BRAW

First published 2014
by Black & White Publishing Ltd
29 Ocean Drive, Edinburgh EH6 6JL

1 3 5 7 9 10 8 6 4 2   14 15 16 17
ISBN: 978 1 91023 002 2

Text copyright © Black & White Publishing Ltd, 2014

Front cover image copyright © Black & White Publishing Ltd, 2014

Broons text © DC Thomson & Co. Ltd. 2014

Recipes copyright © Doreen Culley 2014

Food photographs copyright © Alan Donaldson 2014

The Broons logo and supporting characters (excluding elements listed
in picture credits) appear courtesy of, and are copyright The Broons and
Maw Broon's Kitchen ®© DC Thomson & Co. Ltd. 2014

All rights reserved. No part of this publication may be reproduced,
stored in a retrieval system, or transmitted in any form, or by any means,
electronic, mechanical, photocopying, recording or otherwise, without permission
in writing from the publisher.

A CIP catalogue record for this book is available from the British Library.

Typeset by Stuart Polson Design
Printed and bound in Poland www.hussarbooks.pl

Maw Broon's
Kitchen®

Bake

with
Maw Broon

Assisted by Doreen Culley

Photographs by Alan Donaldson

Black & White Publishing

For afternoon tea

Lovely wee treats

Su

...nner

Perfect for a picnic

Scrumptious scones

Contents

Love
from
Maw
x

Aboot the Author

Maw Broon is the indomitable matriarch of the Broon family and the original domestic goddess. In between cooking, cleaning and setting the world tae rights with a braw cup of tea, she has also found time tae become the bestselling author of *Maw Broon's Cookbook*, *Maw Broon's But an' Ben Cookbook*, *Maw Broon's Afternoon Tea Book* and *Maw Broon's Cooking with Bairns*. *Bake with Maw Broon* is her definitive guide tae guid Scottish home baking. She lives with her husband and eight children at 10 Glebe Street, Auchenshoogle.

Introduction

For as long as I can remember, I've been baking. I've made scrumptious cakes, braw biscuits and perfect pastry for mah hungry family for years and am always up tae mah elbows in flour or stirring bubbling pots o' homemade jam, but it a' started when I used tae help mah ain maw when ah was a wee lassie. I would help tae weigh oot ingredients, stir the mixture (and lick the spoon when she wisnae lookin'!) and then pour it intae a cake tin. It was hard tae fathom that the gloopy-lookin' mix would turn intae a cake, but one o' mah first memories is waitin' by the oven for it tae be ready and no bein' able tae believe mah eyes when mah maw opened the door, reached in wi' her oven gloves and took oot a magnificent cake, perfectly risen and golden-brown on top. And the wonderful smell of freshly baked cake... well, that stays special every time, no matter how old ye are!

It's because I loved baking wi' mah mother so much that I've tried tae pass on mah love o' baking tae mah ain family. Tae me, baking is a' aboot family. It can bring ye a' together, ye can make something fine for special occasions, gie your loved ones a treat, and even bring harmony tae the household: a braw cake never fails tae put a stop tae an argument – if only because a'body's got their mouths full and cannae speak! Mah family love eatin' everything I bake, but knowin' how tae make it means ye can dae it yourself – and once ye ken the basics ye can adjust recipes tae your ain taste. Mah family kens how tae dae it a' – Horace can work oot the weights and measurements; Hen and Joe can lend a strong arm for the mixing; Daphne and Maggie are a dab hand at making sure a recipe is properly baked; and the Twins and the Bairn are always ready tae help wi' icing and decorating! Even Paw can pummel dough and come oot wi' a braw loaf o' bread. And Granpaw: well, he's guid at eatin' it...

I thought it was high time I spread that joy wi' other people and shared mah baking secrets and favourite recipes at last, so that's why I decided tae write this book, Bake with Maw Broon. Inside ye'll find everything ye need tae know aboot baking: take a peek inside mah larder tae find the ingredients ye'll use most often and the equipment ye'll need; there are conversion charts for measurements and temperatures; and throughout the book I've given ye mah top baking secrets! When it comes tae recipes, ye'll find everything from traditional Scottish favourites tae fancy cakes and twists on the classics. I've also been working on making some of mah old recipes even better, so look oot for updated versions of a few favourites! I've split them intae sections: Cakes and Loaves, Cupcakes and Bakes, Puddings, Pastry, Biscuits, Bread, and Sweets and Treats, as well as special sections on Baking wi' Bairns, Gettin' Fancy, and Bits and Bobs! Whatever tickles your fancy, you're sure tae find what you're lookin' for here.

Before ye get stuck in, here's a wee bit of advice: baking is great fun, but there is a bit o' science behind it and there are basic techniques tae master tae ensure ye get great results. Follow the recipes and measurements exactly, so once ye know whit works and why, ye can start experimentin' and adapting recipes tae your ain taste or tae tickle your loved ones' tastebuds. But the most important thing I can tell ye is: enjoy yourself! And get ready tae bake!

Maw Broon's Larder

A well-stocked larder will stand ye in guid stead when ye start baking. Here I've listed some of the most common ingredients used in baking, which you'll find listed in the recipes throughout this book. It's helpful tae understand whit ye're working with and get a sense of why, too. (Horace is the brains o' the family so he's helped me oot wi' some o' the scientific bits – thanks, son!)

Although there are plenty o' sugars and fats listed here, dinnae worry aboot your waistline too much. As long as ye exercise some restraint – and do some proper exercise as well! – and enjoy your baking in moderation, there's no reason not tae enjoy mah recipes as part o' a balanced diet.

Flour

Plain white flour

Simple! Plain flour is soft and fine-textured and is commonly used when making biscuits and pastries. It's the gluten in flour that forms the basis o' your bake. When the proteins in flour combine wi' liquid, the mix becomes elastic and forms a kind of web that traps air pockets in it, giving your mixture structure. However, too much gluten can make a recipe chewy and tough, so that's why plain white flour, which has a low gluten content, is used for cakes. Store flour in an airtight container in a cool place, and try tae use it quickly, as it is best used when it's fresh.

Strong white flour

This is similar tae plain white flour but has a higher gluten content, which makes the dough more elastic, gives a strong, open texture and makes it more suitable for baking bread.

Self-raising white flour

This is also commonly used in baking and is a pre-made combination of plain flour and baking powder, which helps your cakes tae rise. Be warned: if ye store it for a long time, the power of the baking powder will wear off, so check the date on the packet before using. Ye dinnae want your cakes tae be flat as a pancake!

Raising agents

Bicarbonate of soda

Bicarbonate of soda is a raising agent and will help your cakes rise nicely. It works by giving off carbon dioxide when it's combined wi' an acid (for example, cream of tartar, yogurt, buttermilk or milk), which expands your mixture when it's baked in the oven. But be warned: using too much can make your cake taste awfy, and it will also make it peak and then collapse!

Baking powder

Baking powder is another raising agent, but it already includes the acid (usually cream of tartar) in its mixture. Baking powder disnae affect the taste o' your mixture so much as bicarbonate of soda, but it's still best no' tae use too much.

Yeast

Yeast is an essential part of breadmaking: as it divides and multiplies it produces carbon dioxide, which helps bread tae rise. Ye can use live yeast, but mah recipes call for dried, which ye can easily find in the shops.

Sugar

Brown sugar

Brown sugar is damp and adds moistness tae cakes. Store it in a cool, dry place tae stop it from drying oot. It can be made from adding molasses tae caster sugar, which gives it a beautiful caramel colour and flavour. It can also be made by stopping the sugar-refining process before it becomes white. In this case it'll be labelled as 'unrefined', and some people think this type has a better flavour. Brown sugar can be soft or it can be light or dark. Each type has different properties, so use the kind specified in the recipe.

Caster sugar

Caster sugar is finely ground and has smaller crystals than granulated sugar, which means it creams more easily, making it ideal for use in sponge cakes.

Golden caster sugar

This is caster sugar with molasses added tae it, which gives a caramel colour and flavour.

Icing sugar

Icing sugar is the finest sugar ye can get and is ideal for making icing or for dusting over your cakes.

Demerara sugar

Demerara is a natural brown sugar whose caramel flavour occurs naturally, unlike the brown sugars described above, which have molasses added. It's a coarse sugar that's great for sprinkling and for giving added crunch tae crumbles, flapjacks, biscuits and cheesecake bases.

Muscovado sugar

Like demerara sugar, muscovado is an unrefined sugar wi' a natural caramel flavour. It is moist and sticky. Light muscovado sugar has a treacly flavour, but the dark kind is much stronger.

Black treacle

Black treacle is similar tae molasses but is a bit more refined. It is thick and gloopy, wi' a burnt caramel flavour. It'll make your baking moist and gie a dark colour.

Golden syrup

Golden syrup is even sweeter than sugar! It's an inverted sugar syrup that has a caramel flavour and is great for flapjacks.

Honey

Honey is a gorgeous natural ingredient that can be drizzled over a' sorts of cakes and bakes, but it can also be used tae add flavour tae icing and it can even be used in breadmaking (tae 'feed' the yeast and help it grow). If ye have a guid local honey, use it.

Dairy products

Unsalted butter

There's a reason baking recipes call for unsalted butter – salted butter can toughen gluten, which can make your cakes too chewy. Also, strongly salted butters can make your results taste too salty. Unsalted butter lets ye have more control over both taste and texture. Just make sure it's at room temperature before ye use it, so it's easier tae mix.

Milk

Milk moistens your mixture and also adds structure, as it helps the formation of gluten.

Buttermilk

Buttermilk is more acidic than regular milk and is a better raising agent as a result. It also has a tangier flavour than milk. Ye can buy buttermilk in supermarkets now, but if ye cannae find it, ye can make your own by adding 15ml of lemon juice tae 250ml of full fat milk. Stir well and let it stand for five minutes, and then use as it says in the recipe.

Eggs

Eggs have many uses in baking: they can bind a mixture together, add volume or richness, and can be used as thickeners. If size isnae specified in a recipe, UK medium eggs (50g) are a safe bet. Make sure they're at room temperature before ye use them, as they tend tae curdle if they're too cold. If ye forget, ye can put them in a bowl o' tepid water for a few minutes tae warm them up withoot cooking them.

Chocolate

Dark chocolate

A guid dark chocolate should be at least 70% cocoa solids: experiment and find a brand ye like. Dinnae be tempted tae use cheap 'cooking' chocolate as it has low cocoa solid content and might contain vegetable fat, which won't gie ye guid results.

Cocoa powder

Cocoa powder is powdered chocolate and is used in making chocolate cakes. Dinnae confuse cocoa powder with drinking chocolate, which might have sugar and vegetable fats added, as ye won't get the same result. Use a guid brand for a real chocolatey flavour.

Charts, conversions and timings

Folk hae different ovens and different equipment so might measure things differently. A' the temperatures I've used are for non-fan ovens so if you're using a fan oven, reduce the temperature by 10-20°C. I've included some handy conversion charts here tae keep ye straight. When it comes tae measuring oot ingredients, the important thing is nae tae mix the imperial and metric systems. Choose one and stick tae it, otherwise the quantities will be wrong and the recipe won't work. Mah recipes use the metric system.

Set the oven tae the correct temperature, but mind that the temperature of every oven varies a little depending on whether it's gas, electric or fan-assisted. Wi' non-fan-assisted ovens, the hottest part is at the top and the coolest is at the bottom, so it's a guid idea tae put your baking tins on the middle shelf and away from the side, so your bake doesn't burn. Ye can turn baking trays halfway through cooking for a more even bake. Remember tae check if your oven is fan-assisted because then ye'll need tae adjust the temperature accordingly. Fan-assisted ovens circulate heat more evenly and make the whole oven hotter, so that means baking times can be reduced – keep an eye on your bake! Ye can use this test to see if your bake is ready: put a skewer gently into the centre and if it doesn't come oot clean after the recommended time, keep checking every few minutes until it does.

Finally, remember that ovens are hot. If ye're bakin' wi' bairns, never let them put tins in the oven or take them oot – always do it for them. And remember tae put on your oven gloves!

OVEN TEMPERATURES

Gas Mark	°C	Description
1	140	VERY COOL
2	150	COOL
3	170	WARM
4	180	MODERATE
5	190	FAIRLY HOT
6	200	FAIRLY HOT
7	220	HOT
8	230	VERY HOT
9	240	VERY HOT

Volumes

Fluid ounces	Millilitres
1	25
2	55
3	75
4	120
5	150
6	175
7	200
8	225
9	250
10	275
15	425
20/1 pint	570
1¼ pints	725
1½ pints	850
1¾ pints	1 litre

Weights

Ounces	Grams
1	25
2	50
3	75
4	110
5	150
6	175
7	200
8	225
9	250
10	275
11	315
12	350
13	365
14	400
15	425
16/1 lb	450

OTHER MEASURES

1 TEASPOON = 5ML

1 TABLESPOON = 15ML

1

Cakes
and
Loaves

Victoria sponge

Victoria sponge is a true classic and mah light sponge just melts in your mouth. Everyone in the family loves it, and it's the only thing that'll get Horace away from his books – as long the rest of the bairns haven't got tae it first! Sandwiched together with strawberries and cream, it's perfect for any occasion.

Two sandwich 8" round cake tins
Baking paper

For the cake:
3 medium eggs
180g unsalted butter
180g caster sugar
180g self-raising flour

Tae decorate:
300ml whipped cream
300g strawberries, sliced
Icing sugar, tae dust

1. Preheat non-fan oven tae 170°C

2. Grease and line two sandwich 8" round cake tins

3. Break 3 medium eggs and weigh (should be around 170g). NB for the ideal sponge, once ye know the weight of your eggs, adjust the butter, sugar and flour to the same weight

4. Measure equal amounts of butter, sugar and flour

5. Beat butter and sugar together until light and fluffy

6. Add eggs one at a time and mix well

7. Fold in flour until mixture is smooth

8. Divide mixture between two tins

9. Bake in the centre of the oven for 40 minutes or until a skewer inserted intae the centre comes oot clean

10. Cool in the tin for 10 minutes before transferring tae a wire rack tae cool completely

11. Spread whipped cream on bottom half of cake and generously cover with sliced strawberries

12. Place top of cake and dust with icing sugar and decorate wi' strawberries

Tip

Tae decorate wi' buttercream roses:

– Make the basic buttercream recipe – see page 185

– Fill a piping bag and use a 2D Wilton flower nozzle

– Tae pipe the rose design, start from the middle and work oot in a spiral until the cake is covered

– Ye can practise the rose technique on parchment or baking paper first

Chocolate cake

Chocolate cake is oor Daphne's absolute favourite, as it combines twa o' her favourite things: chocolate and cake! The buttermilk and the twa different sugars in mah recipe make it rich and fudgy, and the wee spoonful o' coffee gies it depth o' flavour. Served wi' a dollop o' cream, this chocolate cake is irresistible.

7" round cake tin
Baking paper
Saucepan

200g dark chocolate, broken intae pieces
200g unsalted butter
1 tablespoon instant coffee dissolved in 100ml hot water, then cooled
80g self-raising flour
80g plain flour
½ teaspoon bicarbonate of soda
200g golden caster sugar
200g light muscovado sugar
25g cocoa powder
3 medium eggs
75ml buttermilk

1. Preheat non-fan oven tae 160°C

2. Grease and line a 7" round cake tin

3. In a saucepan add chocolate, butter and coffee mixture and gently mix together over a low heat until smooth

4. In a large mixing bowl, mix together the flours, bicarbonate of soda, sugars and cocoa powder

5. In a separate bowl, beat eggs and buttermilk together

6. Add chocolate mixture and egg mixture tae dried ingredients and mix well until smooth

7. Pour mixture intae prepared tin

8. Bake in the centre of preheated oven for 40 tae 50 minutes or until a skewer inserted intae the centre comes oot clean

9. Leave tae cool in the tin for 20 minutes then transfer tae a wire rack tae cool completely

10. Once cooled, split cake intae 2 and fill wi' chocolate buttercream or chocolate ganache (see pp185/186)

Tip

If the chocolate cake isnae enough on its own, there's plenty ye can dae tae make it even more special. Ye can drizzle it wi' Baileys for a boozy treat, make a chocolatey peanut-butter filling, or even add cherries and whipped cream tae turn it intae a Black Forest gateau.

Baileys – drizzle cake liberally with Baileys and fill with chocolate ganache

Peanut butter – Mix together a jar of peanut butter with a jar of chocolate spread and fill cake

Black Forest – Drizzle cake with some mashed morello cherries and fill wi' whipped cream, pipe whipped cream onto top and grate dark chocolate over

Coffee and walnut loaf

After a hard day's work, Hen likes a slice of mah coffee and walnut loaf when he comes home and settles doon wi' the newspaper – but I suspect he wraps up a wee slice tae tak' tae the office wi' him in the morning as well! He's always got space for a slice. Mah recipe is strong, dark and a bit nutty – just like mah first-born laddie!

1lb loaf tin

100g unsalted butter, softened
150g brown sugar
2 medium eggs
1 heaped teaspoon instant coffee dissolved in 3 tablespoons hot water, then cooled
200g plain flour
½ teaspoon baking powder
80g walnuts, chopped

1. Preheat non-fan oven tae 180°C

2. Grease a 1lb loaf tin

3. In a large bowl, cream the butter and sugar until light and fluffy

4. Add eggs one at a time and mix well

5. Add coffee mixture tae cake batter and mix well

6. Add flour and baking powder and mix until smooth

7. Add walnuts and mix

8. Pour mixture intae your prepared tin

9. Place in the centre of preheated oven for 30 minutes

10. Turn the oven down tae 150°C and bake for a further 30 minutes or until a skewer inserted intae the centre comes oot clean

11. Cool in tin for 10 minutes then cool completely on a wire rack

Dundee cake

This famous Scottish fruit cake is like a taste o' hame. It was first invented by the famous Dundee marmalade manufacturers Keiller's, who gave the cake its special flavour by using crystallised orange peel from its ain marmalade. Paw thinks it goes perfectly wi' a wee dram in front o' a roarin' fire.

8" round cake tin
Baking paper
Electric mixer

150g unsalted butter
150g caster sugar
3 large eggs
225g plain flour
1 teaspoon baking powder
350g mixed dried fruit
50g glacé cherries, halved
50g dried mixed peel
50g ground almonds
Zest of 1 lemon and 1 orange
50g blanched almonds

1. Preheat non-fan oven tae 170°C

2. Grease and double line an 8" round cake tin

3. Cream the butter and sugar together wi' an electric mixer until light and fluffy

4. Add whisked eggs tae the mixture a little at a time until combined

5. Sift flour and baking powder together and fold intae mixture

6. Fold in mixed fruit, cherries, mixed peel, ground almonds and zest until well combined

7. Spoon mixture intae prepared cake tin and carefully flatten wi' the back of a spoon

8. Very carefully place the blanched almonds onto the surface

9. Bake for 2 tae 2½ hours in the centre of the preheated oven

10. Leave cake tae cool in cake tin before transferring tae a wire rack

Tip

Soak your dried fruit in 2 tablespoons of lemon or orange juice or 2 tablespoons of your favourite whisky for 2 hours before making cake

MY, IT'S GRAND TO GET YER FEET UP AN' HAVE A READ AT THE PAPER!

Gingerbread loaf

After practising his boxing, Joe deserves a slice of mah gingerbread loaf while he cools down. Rich, moist and spicy, it's a cake that packs a fair punch! But ye can add always some more sweetness by drizzling a sugar glaze on top.

1lb large loaf tin
Baking paper
Saucepan

115g dark muscovado sugar
115g unsalted butter
115g golden syrup
115g black treacle
225g plain flour
2 teaspoons bicarbonate of soda
2 teaspoons ground cinnamon
2 teaspoons ground ginger
2 medium eggs
30ml milk

1. Preheat non-fan oven tae 180°C

2. Grease and line a 1lb large loaf tin

3. Gently heat sugar, butter, syrup and treacle in a saucepan until smooth and runny

4. In a large bowl add the sifted flour, bicarbonate of soda, cinnamon and ginger

5. Make a well in the middle of the dry ingredients, pour in the melted liquid and mix well

6. Mix in the eggs and milk until mixture is smooth

7. Pour mixture intae prepared loaf tin

8. Bake in preheated oven for 60 minutes or until a skewer inserted intae the centre comes oot clean

9. Leave tae cool in the tin for 10 minutes then cool completely on a wire rack

Tip

Add a glaze tae the top of your cake by mixing 150g icing sugar wi' a little water and drizzling over the loaf

ROOND ANE...

BIFF!

JOE'S STARTED WEEL. HE'S JABBIN' AN' DUCKIN' . . . OH. END O' THE ROOND A'READY.

DING!

Marmalade cake

This sticky, fruity cake is a favourite of the Twins – they cannae get enough o' it! They keep tellin' me because it's got orange and other fruit in it that it must be at least twa o' their five a day, the cheeky scamps. I've forbidden them tae touch it until they've eaten their dinner. I wonder if they've managed tae keep their hands aff?

7" round cake tin
Baking paper

225g plain flour
15g baking powder
125g dark soft brown sugar
125g unsalted butter
1 teaspoon ground mixed spice
125g dried mixed fruit
Zest of 1 orange and 1 lemon
150ml milk
1 teaspoon white wine vinegar
1 large tablespoon marmalade
1 tablespoon demerara sugar

1. Preheat non-fan oven tae 180°C

2. Grease and line a 7" round cake tin

3. Mix flour, baking powder and sugar together in a large mixing bowl

4. Add the butter and rub through your fingers until mixture resembles breadcrumbs

5. Add mixed spice, mixed fruit and zest and mix together

6. Add the milk, a little at a time, and mix well

7. Add white wine vinegar and marmalade and mix well

8. Spoon mixture intae prepared cake tin and flatten wi the back of a spoon

9. Sprinkle demerara sugar onto mixture

10. Bake in the centre of a preheated oven for 1½ hours or until firm tae touch

11. Cool cake in tin before transferring tae a wire rack

Madeira cake

Madeira cake is a wonderful cake tae have in your repertoire. It's a feather-light sponge that's easy tae bake, and ye can add a' sorts o' things tae jazz it up, like glacé cherries, sultanas or even chocolate chips. Oor Maggie likes tae have a slice just before she goes oot tae see her sweetheart – whit an excuse!

8" round cake tin
Baking paper
Electric mixer
Two sheets of newspaper
String

375g plain flour
1½ teaspoons baking powder
325g unsalted butter
325g caster sugar
5 medium eggs
45ml milk or fruit juice

1. Preheat non-fan oven tae 160°C

2. Grease and line an 8" round cake tin with baking paper

3. Add a' ingredients tae a large mixing bowl and mix well wi' an electric mixer until smooth and glossy

4. Place mixture intae prepared tin and flatten with the back of a spoon

5. Fold two sheets of newspaper lengthways three times and wrap around the cake tin and secure wi' string. (The cake takes a bit longer in the oven than other cakes, so the newspaper protects the outer edge from overcooking)

6. Place in the centre of your preheated oven and bake for 1½ hours or until a skewer inserted intae the centre comes oot clean

7. Leave tae cool completely in the tin

Tip

Add 100g of glacé cherries, sultanas or chocolate chips for a twist on the basic recipe

1.

Maw's Top Tips

When baking any cake, always line your tin before
putting the mixture in. Grease the tin and line it
with baking paper or, if you don't have any paper
to hand, coat it with flour. This way, the cake
will come out smoothly in one piece
once it's cooled!

Gluten-free Madeira cake

Some poor souls are intolerant o' gluten, so here's a special recipe for them. It uses ground almonds and gluten-free flour, so there's nae need tae miss oot on this marvellous cake.

1lb large loaf tin
Baking paper

150g unsalted butter
150g caster sugar
50g ground almonds
100g gluten-free self-raising flour
3 medium eggs
30ml milk
Zest of 1 lemon or orange

1. Preheat non-fan oven tae 170°C

2. Grease and line a 1lb large loaf tin

3. Add a' ingredients tae a large mixing bowl and mix until smooth and glossy

4. Add mixture tae prepared cake tin and flatten wi' the back of a spoon

5. Bake in the centre of your preheated oven for a minimum of 60 minutes, or until a skewer inserted intae the centre comes oot clean

6. Cool completely in tin

Banana loaf

The Twins love mah banana loaf: soft, dense and packed full of fruity goodness, it sees them through a hard day's playing! They always mind and pick up the skins after I've peeled the bananas, too. Now what mischief could they be up tae?

1lb large loaf tin
Baking paper

200g plain flour
½ teaspoon bicarbonate of soda
1 teaspoon baking powder
115g caster sugar
60g unsalted butter, softened
2 ripe bananas, mashed
1 medium egg
1 tablespoon milk

1. Preheat non-fan oven tae 180°C

2. Grease and line a 1lb large loaf tin

3. Sift flour, bicarbonate of soda and baking powder intae a large bowl

4. Add sugar and butter and rub through mixture using your hands, until mixture resembles breadcrumbs

5. Add bananas, egg and milk and mix well wi' a wooden spoon

6. Pour mixture intae prepared loaf tin

7. Bake in the centre of your preheated oven for 60 minutes or until golden-brown

8. Leave tae cool in the tin for 10 minutes then cool completely on a wire rack

Honey and whisky cake

This honey and whisky cake is one of mah specialities and it goes down a treat, especially wi' the Broon menfolk. I've just made one for a coffee morning and Granpaw said he'd drap it aff on his way tae the allotments. I wonder if he's delivered it yet? Somehow I dinnae think it'll get there in one piece because there's always something going on at his gairden!

Two 6" round cake tins
Baking paper
Electric mixer

For the cake:
170g unsalted butter
170g soft brown sugar
Zest of one orange
3 medium eggs
50ml your chosen whisky (blended is fine)
170g self-raising flour

For the buttercream:
170g icing sugar
60g unsalted butter, softened
2 tablespoons local honey
1 teaspoon orange juice

1. Preheat non-fan oven tae 190°C

2. Grease and line two 6" round cake tins

3. In a large mixing bowl, cream the butter and sugar until light and fluffy

4. Add orange zest and mix in eggs, one at a time

5. Add whisky and half the flour and fold in until incorporated

6. Add remaining flour and fold gently until smooth

7. Split mixture between tins and flatten with the back of a spoon

8. Bake in your preheated oven for 25 minutes or until golden-brown

9. Cool in tin for 10 minutes before transferring tae a wire rack tae cool completely

For the buttercream:

1. In a large bowl, add the sugar, butter and honey and mix well wi' an electric mixer, then add the teaspoon of orange juice and mix until light and fluffy

2. Sandwich cakes together wi' the buttercream and sprinkle the top wi' a little icing sugar

Lemon drizzle loaf

Mah lemon drizzle loaf is a lovely light sponge tae enjoy on a fresh spring day. Sharp like lemon and sweet like sugar, it's a cake the whole family can enjoy when we go off tae the But 'n' Ben for the weekend.

Two 1lb large loaf tins
Baking paper

175g unsalted butter, softened
175g caster sugar
Zest and juice of 2 unwaxed lemons
3 medium eggs
100g self-raising flour
75g ground almonds
A little milk
80g demerara sugar, tae sprinkle

1. Preheat non-fan oven tae 180°C
2. Grease and line two 1lb large loaf tins
3. Cream butter, sugar and zest of both lemons until light and fluffy
4. Add eggs one at a time and mix well
5. Fold in flour and almonds until mixture is smooth
6. Add a little milk at a time until the mixture reaches pouring consistency
7. Spoon mixture intae prepared tins
8. Bake in the centre of the oven for 55 tae 60 minutes or until a skewer inserted intae the centre comes oot clean
9. Mix the juice of both lemons wi' the demerara sugar and drizzle over the warm loaves

2

Cupcakes
and
Bakes

Basic cupcakes

Cupcakes are perfect for a big family like oors – there's one for everybody, and there's no fightin' ower who's got the biggest slice! There are endless possibilities wi' cupcakes too: ye can fill them wi' chocolate or Caramac, or even turn them intae mini banoffee pies. I sometimes put mah jam-filled cupcakes intae the Twins' lunchboxes as a wee treat.

12-hole muffin tray
12 muffin-sized paper cases
Piping bag with a star nozzle

For the cupcakes:
180g unsalted butter
180g caster sugar
3 medium eggs
180g self-raising flour

Tae decorate:
1x basic buttercream recipe

1. Preheat non-fan oven tae 170°C
2. Place 12 muffin-sized paper cases intae a muffin tray
3. Beat the butter and sugar until light and fluffy
4. Add eggs a little at a time and mix well
5. Mix in flour until mixture is smooth and glossy
6. Divide mixture between 12 cases
7. Bake in the oven for 25 minutes or until golden-brown
8. Cool cupcakes on a wire rack
9. Prepare basic buttercream recipe (see p185)
10. Using a piping bag with a star nozzle, pipe a swirl on top of cupcake

Optional fillings

Jam – Before piping buttercream onto cupcake, remove centre of cupcake using an apple corer. Fill wi' jam of your choice

Caramac – Before piping buttercream onto cupcake, remove centre of cupcake using an apple corer and fill with caramel sauce (see p187). Sprinkle some broken Caramac chocolate on top of buttercream and finish off with a drizzle of caramel sauce

Banoffee – Add a couple of slices of banana tae the top of piped cake, drizzle wi' caramel sauce and finish with a sprinkle of grated chocolate

Chocolate-bar centre – Remove cupcakes from oven after 25 minutes and then, using a sharp knife, cut a cross intae each cupcake and insert a slice of your favourite chocolate bar. Return tae the oven for 5 minutes tae melt

2.
Maw's Top Tips

Always preheat your oven before ye start. The cakes won't bake right if you put them in while the oven is still heating up. Also, dinnae slam the oven door when you're checking the cake, because it fills the oven wi' cold air really quickly. It will take 10 minutes tae reheat again, so close it gently.

Chocolate cupcakes

How can ye improve on mah basic cupcake recipe? By adding chocolate, of course! These are like mini versions of mah melt-in-the-mouth chocolate cake and as soon as they're oot of the oven they go like... well... like hot cakes! But if ye can wait for them tae cool and get icing piped on them, you'll be in chocolate heaven.

12-hole muffin tray
12 muffin-sized paper cases
Saucepan

For the cupcakes:
50g unsalted butter, softened
100g dark chocolate, broken intae pieces
120ml milk
30g cocoa powder
100g unsalted butter, softened
150g golden caster sugar
1 large egg
½ teaspoon vanilla extract
1 teaspoon instant coffee dissolved in 1 tablespoon hot water, then cooled
110g self-raising flour

Tae decorate:
1x chocolate buttercream or chocolate ganache recipe

1. Preheat non-fan oven tae 180°C

2. Place 12 muffin-sized cupcake cases intae a muffin tray

3. In a saucepan, gently melt 50g butter, chocolate, milk and cocoa, stirring until well combined

4. Cream 100g butter and sugar together in a bowl until light and fluffy

5. Add egg and vanilla tae the butter mixture and mix thoroughly

6. Pour in chocolate mixture and coffee mixture and mix well

7. Fold in flour until smooth and glossy

8. Divide between the cupcake cases

9. Bake in preheated oven for 20 tae 25 minutes

10. Cool cupcakes on a wire rack

11. Decorate with chocolate buttercream or chocolate ganache

Cupcakes in a jar

This is a lovely way tae turn your cupcakes intae a wonderful, eye-catching present for someone ye love. Oor Maggie is a right one for watching her figure, but even she couldnae resist these bonny cupcakes! And if you're a dainty soul, ye dinnae even have tae get your hands dirty: just eat them oot the jar wi' a spoon. A real treat for a relaxing afternoon.

Clear jam jars with a lid (1 jar per 2 cupcakes used)
Piping bag with star nozzle
Ribbon
Gift tag
Spoon

2 cupcakes per jar
Buttercream

1. Divide each cupcake in two
2. Place one layer of cupcake intae the bottom of the jar
3. Spoon on jam of your choice
4. Pipe a swirl of buttercream
5. Place a layer of cupcake
6. Repeat layering until ye reach the top of the jar
7. Secure lid
8. Tie ribbon around neck of jar, securing gift tag and spoon

53

3.

Maw's Top Tips

Clean your oven regularly tae prevent any smells from contaminating your baking. If ye need tae use cleaning products, wipe the oven doon wi' warm soapy water once you're done. After that, ye can steam the oven by putting a heatproof bowl or tin filled wi' water in tae cook for aboot ten minutes. That'll remove any remaining smells.

Pecan and maple syrup cupcakes

Pecan nuts and maple syrup are a match made in heaven, so I decided tae try them oot in a cupcake. Jings! They were so delicious a' the family scoffed them before I could serve them tae mah cronies for afternoon tea! Ach weel, I'll just hae tae bake some more . . .

12-hole muffin tray
12 muffin-sized paper cases

For cupcakes:
125g unsalted butter
100g caster sugar
75g dark brown sugar
2 medium eggs, beaten
2 tablespoons maple syrup
175g self-raising flour

Tae decorate:
1x basic buttercream recipe
Chopped pecans, tae sprinkle
Maple syrup, tae drizzle

1. Preheat non-fan oven tae 180°C
2. Place 12 muffin-sized paper cases intae a muffin tray
3. Beat the butter and sugars until light and fluffy
4. Add eggs a little at a time and mix well
5. Add maple syrup and mix well
6. Mix in flour until mixture is smooth and glossy
7. Divide mixture between 12 cases
8. Bake in the oven for 20 minutes or until golden-brown
9. Decorate wi' basic buttercream recipe
10. Sprinkle wi' chopped pecans
11. Drizzle wi' a little maple syrup

Chocolate brownies

Well, if I thought Daphne was a fan o' mah chocolate cake, wait until she got hold of mah rich, fudgy brownies! She took a plateful awa' wi' her, tae keep her goin' during her sewing, she said. She'll hae tae watch oot or else she'll have tae let oot that dressmaker's dummy! Always eat sensibly!

7" square cake tin

Baking paper

Saucepan

115g unsalted butter

115g dark chocolate, broken intae pieces

300g caster sugar

Pinch of salt

1 teaspoon vanilla extract

2 large eggs

140g plain flour

2 tablespoons cocoa powder

100g white chocolate chips

1. Preheat non-fan oven tae 180°C

2. Grease and line a 7" square cake tin

3. Place butter and dark chocolate in a saucepan and stir over a low heat until melted

4. Remove from heat and stir until smooth

5. Stir in the sugar, salt and vanilla

6. Add the eggs one at a time and mix well

7. Sift the flour and cocoa over the mixture and beat until smooth

8. Stir in the white chocolate chips

9. Pour mixture intae prepared cake tin

10. Bake in the oven for 35 tae 40 minutes until a skewer inserted intae the centre comes oot almost clean

11. Cool completely on a wire rack

12. Cut intae squares

Raspberry and white chocolate blondies

If normal brownies made with dark chocolate aren't tae your taste, never fear: here are mah raspberry and white chocolate blondies instead. Soft, dense and squidgy, these sweet treats are ideal for a summer's day.

8" square cake tin
Baking paper
Saucepan

115g unsalted butter
200g white chocolate, chopped intae small pieces
2 medium eggs
115g caster sugar
125g plain flour
115g fresh raspberries

1. Preheat non-fan oven tae 190°C

2. Grease and line an 8" square cake tin

3. In a saucepan, melt the butter and half the chocolate, stir until smooth and remove from the heat

4. In a large bowl, whisk the eggs and sugar until thick and creamy

5. Add the flour and melted chocolate and butter and fold intae the mixture

6. Add the raspberries and remaining chocolate and very gently fold intae mixture

7. Bake in preheated oven for 40 tae 50 minutes or until golden-brown

8. Cool in the tin before cutting intae squares

Paris buns

Ye dinnae hae tae go a' the way tae Paris tae get these tasty buns – despite their name, they actually come from Scotland and Ireland. The sweet, soft dough makes a fine contrast wi' the crunchy sugar topping. Get as fancy as ye like wi' the coloured sugar. Ooh la la!

Two baking trays
Baking paper

For the buns:
115g unsalted butter
125g caster sugar
2 tablespoons malt powder
½ teaspoon bicarbonate of soda
2 medium eggs
150ml buttermilk
250g plain flour
2 teaspoons baking powder

Tae decorate:
Coloured sugar, tae sprinkle

1. Preheat non-fan oven tae 220°C

2. Line two baking trays

3. Cream the butter and sugar together until light and fluffy

4. Add the malt powder and bicarbonate of soda and mix well

5. Add eggs and buttermilk and mix until mixture reaches a batter consistency (it may look curdled)

6. Sift in the flour and baking powder and mix until a soft dough forms

7. Using a tablespoon, spoon rough balls onto the trays, spaced well apart. The buns will spread while baking

8. Sprinkle balls with coloured sugar

9. Bake in a preheated oven for 12 tae 15 minutes until golden-brown

10. Cool on a wire rack

Scones

Scotland might be famous for the Stone of Scone, but let me assure ye that mah scones are light as a feather! I often treat maself tae a scone while I'm takin' a break from mah knittin'. I love them whether spread wi' butter or piled wi' clotted cream and strawberry jam. And adding a handful o' sultanas or glacé cherries turns them intae a fruity treat. But mind and don't forget that they're in the oven!

Two baking trays
Baking paper
Round or fluted pastry cutter
Pastry brush

450g plain flour
2 teaspoons baking powder
½ teaspoon salt
55g unsalted butter, cubed
2 teaspoons caster sugar
250ml milk

1. Preheat non-fan oven tae 220°C

2. Line two baking trays with baking paper

3. Sift flour, baking powder and salt intae a large bowl

4. Add butter and rub intae mixture until it resembles breadcrumbs

5. Stir in sugar

6. Gradually add milk until the mixture becomes a soft dough (ye may not need a' the milk)

7. Roll oot dough mixture onto a lightly floured surface until around 1½" in thickness

8. Cut oot scones wi' a round or fluted pastry cutter and place onto prepared baking trays

9. Brush the top of the scones with a little milk

10. Bake in the preheated oven for 10 tae 12 minutes or until golden-brown

11. Cool on a wire rack or serve hot

Tip

Fruit scones
– add 55g of sultanas

Cherry scones
– add 55g of washed, halved glacé cherries

Blueberry scones
– add 55g of fresh blueberries

Cranachan scones

Cranachan, that rich mix of fresh raspberries, peaty whisky, crunchy oatmeal, sweet honey and whipped cream, is mah favourite dessert, so I decided tae combine it wi' mah other favourite: scones! The result is the best o' both worlds: an indulgent tea-party treat that'll knock the socks off your pals.

Two baking trays
Baking paper
Round or fluted pastry cutter
Pastry brush

450g self-raising flour
Pinch of salt
85g unsalted butter, cubed
50g caster sugar
100g oatmeal
2 tablespoons local honey
Tablespoon of your favourite whisky (optional)
150ml milk, tae glaze

For filling:
Fresh raspberries and whipped cream

1. Preheat non-fan oven tae 200°C
2. Line two baking trays with baking paper
3. Sift flour and salt together intae a large bowl
4. Add butter and rub in through fingertips until mixture resembles breadcrumbs
5. Stir in sugar and oatmeal
6. Add honey and whisky, if using. Knead mixture
7. Gradually add milk until the mixture becomes a soft dough (ye may not need a' the milk)
8. Roll oot mixture on a lightly floured surface until approximately 2cm thick
9. Cut oot scones using a round or fluted pastry cutter and place on trays
10. Brush tops of scones wi' a little milk
11. Bake in a preheated oven for 12 tae 15 minutes or until golden-brown
12. Cool on a wire rack
13. Serve wi' fresh raspberries and whipped cream

Cheese scones

Cheese scones are a delicious savoury twist on mah plain scones. The tart Cheddar cheese perfectly complements the rich butteriness o' the dough, making a mouthwatering treat for those who dinnae hae such a sweet tooth. Ye can even serve them alongside a hearty bowl o' soup as an alternative tae bread.

Two baking trays
Baking paper
Round or fluted pastry cutter
Pastry brush

450g plain flour
2 teaspoons baking powder
½ teaspoon salt
55g unsalted butter, cubed
55g Cheddar cheese, grated
250ml milk

1. Preheat non-fan oven tae 220°C

2. Line two baking trays with baking paper

3. Sift flour, baking powder and salt intae a large bowl

4. Add butter and rub intae the mixture until it resembles breadcrumbs

5. Stir in cheese

6. Gradually add milk until the mixture becomes a soft dough (ye may not need a' the milk)

7. Roll oot dough mixture onto a lightly floured surface until around 1½ " in thickness

8. Cut oot scones wi' a round or fluted pastry cutter and place onto prepared baking trays

9. Brush the top of the scones with a little milk

10. Bake in the preheated oven for 10 tae 12 minutes or until golden-brown

11. Cool on a wire rack or serve hot

Puddings

Bread and butter pudding

Bread and butter pudding is a guid rib-sticking pudding. Oor Joe eats it by the bowlful tae build himself up – or so he says! Though it sounds simple, there are lots of things ye can dae tae turn it intae something special: for example, ye can change the type o' bread and use different fruits. Sprinkled wi' sugar and served wi' cream, it's delicious.

Shallow baking dish
Measuring jug

80g sultanas
Several slices of stale bread, fruit loaf or brioche
40g unsalted butter
60ml single cream
450ml milk
2 medium eggs, plus additional egg yolk
Brown sugar
Ground nutmeg
Ground cinnamon

1. Soak sultanas in a little boiling water for a few minutes until soft, then drain
2. Butter a shallow baking dish
3. Spread the bread slices wi' the butter
4. Lay slices in dish, overlapping each one
5. Evenly sprinkle the sultanas over the bread
6. In a large measuring jug, add the cream and make up tae a pint with the milk
7. Add the eggs and egg yolk tae the milk and whisk
8. Pour over the bread evenly
9. Sprinkle wi' brown sugar, cinnamon and nutmeg
10. Place in fridge and leave for an hour
11. Preheat non-fan oven tae 175°C
12. Place in the preheated oven for 45 minutes
13. Eat warm wi' cream

Tip

For a really posh twist, use mah Selkirk bannock instead of bread

Fruit crumble

This is a pudding ye can make a' year round, depending on whit fruits are in season. In summer, think aboot strawberries, raspberries, blueberries and blackberries; in winter, turn tae apples, plums and pears. What never changes, though, is the sugary, crunchy crumble topping: always delicious no matter what's underneath!

9" ovenproof pie dish

For the filling:
1kg ripe summer fruits
225g caster sugar
2 teaspoons lemon juice
1 tablespoon cornflour
1 teaspoon mixed spice

For the crumble topping:
150g plain flour
110g brown sugar
½ tsp cinnamon
1 teaspoon baking powder
Pinch of salt
110g unsalted butter, cubed

1. Preheat non-fan oven tae 190°C

2. In a large mixing bowl add fruit, sugar, lemon juice, cornflour and mixed spice and toss until a' fruit is coated

3. Pour intae a 9" ovenproof pie dish and set aside

4. In a large mixing bowl mix together the flour, sugar, cinnamon, baking powder and salt

5. Add butter and rub through fingers until large crumbs are formed

6. Pour crumble topping mix evenly over fruit

7. Bake in preheated oven for 35 minutes

8. Leave tae cool for at least 20 minutes before serving

Sticky toffee and date pudding

This is a soft sponge pudding stuffed wi' dates and drenched in toffee sauce. There are always sticky fingers and faces after oor family's done wi' it, from lickin' the plate! Served wi' vanilla ice cream, this is a pudding that's hard tae beat.

Large ovenproof pudding bowl

For the pudding:
110g dark muscovado sugar
180g self-raising flour
120ml milk
1 large egg
1 teaspoon vanilla extract
50g unsalted butter, melted
220g dates, chopped

For the sauce:
200g dark muscovado sugar
30g unsalted butter, cubed
500ml boiling water

1. Preheat non-fan oven tae 190°C
2. Grease a large ovenproof pudding bowl
3. In a large mixing bowl combine sugar and flour
4. Whisk together milk, egg, vanilla and melted butter
5. Pour liquid over flour mixture and combine
6. Fold in dates
7. Add mixture tae an ovenproof pudding bowl
8. To make sauce, sprinkle the remaining dark muscovado sugar over mixture
9. Add cubed butter tae top of mixture
10. Pour boiling water over top – it looks like a lot of water but this will turn into the sauce
11. Place in the centre of the oven for 50 tae 60 minutes
12. Flip pudding onto a plate and serve wi' vanilla ice cream or cream

Jam roly-poly

I always say, if ye eat too much of this ye'll end up roly-poly, and then ye'll be in a jam! But who cares when it's this delicious? This classic pudding is a firm favourite wi' us Broons, especially when it's served wi' thick yellow custard.

Baking dish
Cling film
Rolling pin
Pastry brush
Silicon baking paper
Baking tray

430g plain flour
1 teaspoon baking powder
120g shredded suet
90g unsalted butter, melted
100ml milk (ye may not need a' the milk)
170g warmed jam
A little milk
1 egg yolk, beaten
A little demerara sugar, tae sprinkle

1. Preheat non-fan oven tae 200°C

2. Fill a baking dish with an inch or two of water and place in the bottom of the oven

3. Sift the flour and baking powder intae a large mixing bowl

4. Add the suet, melted butter and enough milk tae create a soft, but not sticky, dough

5. On a lightly floured surface, knead the dough for about 10 minutes or until soft, tae activate the dough

6. Place dough intae a bowl and cover wi' cling film. Leave in fridge for 30 minutes

7. Turn oot dough onto a lightly floured surface and gently knead for a few moments

8. Flour worktop and roll oot a rectangle approximately 12"x8" and around ¼" thick

9. Brush jam over pastry, leaving 1cm border around a' edges

10. Brush milk over border tae help seal the pudding

11. Roll pastry away from ye, being careful not tae push a' the jam tae the end, pinching and folding over edges as ye go

12. Place the roll on a piece of buttered silicon baking paper, sealed side down. The paper needs tae be big enough tae cover the pastry, make space for it tae expand and also so ye can twist the ends later

13. Brush the pudding wi' a little beaten egg yolk and sprinkle with a little demerara sugar

14. Wrap paper over pastry and twist ends like a sweetie wrapper

15. Place the pudding onto a baking tray

16. Bake in the preheated oven for 40 tae 50 minutes

17. Cool for around 15 tae 20 minutes before removing from paper and slicing

4.
Maw's Top Tips

Mah cheesecake recipe doesn't involve any baking, so it's as simple as it can possibly be. But you should still pay attention tae the details tae get a scrumptious, dreamy cheesecake. Did ye ken it's easier tae achieve a smooth, creamy texture if ye whisk the cream cheese when it's at room temperature?

No-bake cheesecake

There's never a crumb left of this rich cheesecake once oor family's finished wi' it! The rich, creamy filling is a perfect foil for the crunchy biscuit base, and juicy summer strawberries set it off nicely. Truly scrumptious. Maybe it'll cheer Paw up a bit!

10" loose-bottomed cake tin
Baking paper

Base:
400g digestive biscuits, crushed
200g unsalted butter, melted

Filling:
500g cream cheese
770g condensed milk
250ml whipped cream

Tae decorate:
Strawberries, sliced

1. Grease and line a 10" loose-bottomed cake tin

2. Combine crushed biscuits and butter wi' a wooden spoon

3. Tip intae prepared cake tin

4. Whisk cream cheese until soft and creamy

5. Add condensed milk and whisk until well mixed and smooth

6. In a separate bowl, whip the cream and then fold intae cream cheese and condensed milk mixture

7. Pour over the base and level wi' the back of a spoon

8. Place in fridge overnight tae set

9. Decorate with sliced strawberries

10. Remove from tin and carefully remove baking paper

73

Tipsy laird

Oor very ain tipsy laird, Granpaw, is a terrible one for this pudding. He's always asking for it – and sometimes I hear him! It's a Scottish take on a trifle: slices of whisky-soaked Victoria sponge are layered wi' raspberries, bananas, whipped cream and, of course, thick yellow custard, then sprinkled wi' cherries. An' Granpaw always insists on havin' a wee dram on the side . . .

Large glass bowl

1x Victoria sponge, sliced
300g raspberry jam
100ml sherry
2 tablespoons whisky
300g raspberries
2 bananas, sliced
1 pint custard
250ml whipped cream
glacé cherries

1. In a large glass bowl, line base wi' sponge slices and spread with raspberry jam

2. Pour whisky and sherry over sponge slices and allow tae soak

3. Add raspberries and bananas

4. Pour custard over fruit layer and level wi' a spoon

5. Smooth whipped cream over custard

6. Decorate with glacé cherries

75

Baked rice pudding

On dreich days – and we do have the occasional one here in Auchenshoogle – there's nothing like a soft, milky rice pudding, fragrant with cinnamon. It's rea[l] comfort food and so easy tae make.

Ovenproof dish
Tin foil

40g pudding rice
25g caster sugar
Knob of unsalted butter
½ teaspoon ground cinnamon
1 teaspoon vanilla extract
650ml milk

1. Preheat non-fan oven tae 160°C

2. Put rice, sugar, butter, cinnamon, vanilla and milk intae an ovenproof dish and stir well

3. Cover dish wi' foil and place in preheated oven fo[r] 30 minutes

4. Remove cover and stir well

5. Return tae oven with the cover off and bake for a further 90 minutes

6. Leave tae cool for 10 minutes before serving

Clootie dumpling

This easy-peasy recipe for clootie dumpling makes this Scottish pudding a doddle! It tak's its name from the cloot (or 'cloth', if you're bein' posh) in which it was traditionally boiled, but I just bake mine in a tin in the oven and it comes oot braw. It's a spicy, fruity treat for a' the family.

2lb loaf tin
Large saucepan

120g unsalted butter
120g caster sugar
360g mixed dried fruit
240g self-raising flour
1 teaspoon bicarbonate of soda
½ teaspoon cream of tartar
1 teaspoon mixed spice
2 medium eggs, beaten

1. Add the butter, sugar and mixed fruit tae a large saucepan. Mix together over a low heat until well combined

2. Remove from heat and allow tae cool

3. Preheat non-fan oven tae 180°C

4. Pour the cooled mixture into a large bowl and add flour, bicarbonate of soda, cream of tartar, mixed spice and eggs and mix together well

5. Place in an oiled 2lb loaf tin and bake in the centre of the preheated oven for 1¼ hours

6. Cool on a wire rack or slice while still hot

4

Pastry

Flaky pastry

Flaky pastry can be tricky tae make, but its buttery flavour and unique texture make it worth the effort.

Large bowl
Rolling pin
Cling film

250g plain flour
250g unsalted butter, at room temperature, cubed
1 teaspoon salt
150ml water

1. In a large bowl, add flour, butter and salt and rub together loosely tae form large crumbs wi' butter pieces still visible

2. Make a well and pour in half the water, then mix together

3. Continue adding a little water at a time until a dough is formed (ye may not need a' the water)

4. Knead the dough on a lightly floured surface, being careful not tae overwork – pieces of butter should still be visible

5. Roll dough in one direction only tae form a rectangle shape approximately 8" by 20", keeping edges level and square

6. Visually divide the dough intae three and fold right side over the centre and then the left side over

7. Cover wi' cling film and rest for 30 minutes

8. Gie the dough a ¼ turn, so that open edges are at the sides, and roll oot again tae previous size. Fold again as before and chill for ten minutes.

9. Repeat the above step one more time, so the pastry will have been folded three times in total, then rest before use.

Sweet pastry

Sweet pastry is enriched with eggs and caster sugar, and is used for a' kinds of sweet tarts and flans.

Large bowl
Cling film
Rolling pin

125g unsalted butter, softened
125g caster sugar
1 medium egg
250g plain flour
Pinch of salt

1. In a large bowl, add the butter and sugar. Mix well together wi' a wooden spoon

2. Add the egg and mix until completely combined

3. Add the flour and a pinch of salt, mix together until combined and a dough is formed

4. Wrap tightly in cling film and place in the fridge for at least 30 minutes

5. When ready tae use your pastry, remove from fridge and leave for 30 minutes at room temperature

6. Roll oot on a lightly floured surface tae desired thickness

Tips

Work quickly and dinnae over handle, as the heat generated will affect the pastry.

Make extra and freeze for later.

Strawberry tart

A strawberry tart is ideal for summertime. After a busy day at the But 'n' Ben, we spread oot the picnic blanket and a'body is lickin' their lips waitin' for this tae be brought oot!

10" loose-bottomed tart tin
Rolling pin
Baking paper
Baking beans or ceramic baking balls

For the base:
1x sweet pastry recipe

For the filling:
600ml whipped cream
600g fresh strawberries, sliced
1x strawberry sauce recipe

1. Preheat non-fan oven tae 190°C

2. On a lightly floured surface roll oot pastry tae approximately ¼" thick

3. Carefully line a 10" loose-bottomed tart tin wi' pastry

4. Chill for 30 minutes

5. Line pastry wi' baking paper and baking beans

6. Bake for 15 minutes, then remove paper and beans and bake for a further 5 minutes

7. Once cooled, remove the pastry from the tin

8. Fill pastry wi' whipped cream and decorate generously with sliced strawberries

9. Drizzle strawberry sauce (see p187) over tart and serve

5.
Maw's Top Tips

Here's a tip for lining tartlet tins wi' your pastry: use your rolling pin tae lift up the rolled-oot pastry, then slide it intae the centre o' the tartlet tin well and lightly press it in wi' a small piece o' excess pastry to avoid tearing. Try no' tae stretch the pastry and then trim off any extra wi' a sharp knife.

Ecclefechan tarts

Named after the village where they were invented, Ecclefechan tarts are stuffed wi' fruit: try sultanas, cherries and currants. Some people serve these tarts at Christmas as an alternative tae mince pies (I say why choose – hae both!) but I think they're braw anytime, especially served warm wi' ice cream.

12-well tartlet tin
Rolling pin

For the base:
1x sweet pastry recipe

For the filling:
120g unsalted butter, melted
180g soft brown sugar
2 medium eggs, beaten
1 tablespoon white wine vinegar
240g dried mixed fruit
60g walnuts, chopped

1. Preheat non-fan oven tae 190°C

2. Lightly grease a 12-well tartlet tin

3. On a lightly floured surface roll oot pastry tae approximately ½ cm thick

4. Cut oot 3" circles and line tartlet tin in each individual cup

5. In a mixing bowl combine the butter, sugar and beaten eggs

6. Add the white wine vinegar, fruit and walnuts and mix well

7. Place a teaspoon of mixture intae each case

8. Bake in a preheated oven for 15 minutes or until golden brown

85

Pumpkin and pecan pie

Pumpkin and pecan pie might be American, but we cannae get enough o' it here at 10 Glebe Street. This sweet, nutty pie is popular wi' a'body at Halloween, and ye could even use the inside o' your carved pumpkins tae make the fillin'. The Twins might get up tae their auld tricks, but this is a proper treat!

9" loose-bottomed tart tin
Rolling pin

For the pastry:
1x sweet pastry recipe

For the filling:
100g caster sugar
100g soft dark brown sugar
1 teaspoon plain flour
¼ teaspoon ground cinnamon
¼ teaspoon ground nutmeg
½ teaspoon salt
2 medium eggs
397g tin of condensed milk
500g pureed pumpkin

For the topping:
80g pecans
30g unsalted butter
60g soft brown sugar
Zest of 1 orange

1. Preheat non-fan oven tae 190°C

2. On a lightly floured surface roll oot pastry tae approximately ¼" thick

3. Carefully line a 9" loose-bottomed tart tin wi' pastry

4. Chill for 30 minutes in fridge

5. In a bowl, mix sugars, flour, spices and salt

6. Add eggs, pureed pumpkin and condensed milk and mix well

7. Pour intae prepared pastry case

8. Bake in preheated oven for 10 minutes

9. Reduce temperature tae 180°C and bake for a further 50 minutes

10. Mix pecans, butter, sugar and orange zest together in a food processor and sprinkle over pie 10 minutes before removing from the oven

87

6.
Maw's Top Tips

Glazing the top of your pie with beaten egg will make it shine and help it turn that appetising golden-brown colour. And making two holes in the crust with a knife before ye put it in the oven will let oot the steam that the rhubarb makes when it's cooking, so your pie won't go soggy.

Rhubarb pie

Rhubarb is a funny old thing: it can be sharp and sweet both at once, and although it's really a vegetable it's usually treated like a fruit! But I've found the perfect home for it in mah rhubarb pie: cooked down wi' sugar, the rhubarb becomes tender and toothsome and makes a braw filling for the sweet pastry.

8" round tart tin

Rolling pin

For the base and lid:
1x sweet pastry recipe

For the filling:
750g rhubarb, sliced
250g caster sugar
1 medium egg, beaten, tae glaze

1. Preheat non-fan oven tae 180°C

2. On a lightly floured surface, roll oot the pastry tae approximately 3mm thick

3. Carefully line the tart tin wi' the pastry and remove excess from the edges

4. Cut the rhubarb intae ½ cm slices

5. Place the rhubarb in the lined tin

6. Sprinkle the sugar over the rhubarb

7. Roll oot remaining pastry and lay over the pie, removing the excess and sealing the edges wi' a little water

8. Cut two holes in the centre of the lid

9. Brush wi' the beaten egg

10. Place in the centre of a preheated oven for 50 tae 60 minutes or until golden-brown

11. Remove from oven and serve

Pigs' lugs

Now, I'll admit that pigs' lugs dinnae sound very appetising – but dinnae worry, they're no' the real thing! These are actually delicious glazed flaky pastry bites sprinkled wi' caster sugar. The Twins love a' things grisly and gruesome so they gobble these up wi' glee, but really pigs' lugs are sugar, spice and a' things nice. Although they don't help with the Twins' hearing!

Baking tray
Baking paper
Rolling pin

1x flaky pastry recipe
Caster sugar, tae sprinkle
100g icing sugar

1. Preheat non-fan oven tae 200°C

2. Line a baking tray wi' baking paper

3. Roll oot pastry on a lightly floured surface tae approximately 10" square

4. Sprinkle your work surface wi' some caster sugar and place your sheet of pastry on top

5. Sprinkle more caster sugar onto the top of the pastry and roll oot a little tae make the sugar stick

6. Fold each side of the pastry intae the centre

7. Repeat the folding step once more

8. Cut the folded pastry intae slices 5mm thick

9. Dip one side of each pastry slice intae some caster sugar and place on the prepared baking tray sugared-side down

10. Bake in the centre of the oven for 10 minutes

11. Remove from the oven and quickly flip each slice over

12. Return the tray tae the oven and bake for a further 5 minutes

13. Remove from oven and allow tae cool completely on a wire rack

14. In a medium-sized bowl, add a' the icing sugar and then a little water at a time until the mixture reaches a runny consistency

15. Dip one side of each pastry intae the icing and allow tae dry icing-side-up on a wire rack

HO!! I THOCHT I TOLD YE I DIDNAE WANT TAE CATCH YE BOUNCIN' ON YER BEDS!

WEEL, IF YE'D STOP CREEPIN' UP ON US, YE WOULDNAE CATCH US, WOULD YE?

7.

Maw's Top Tips

When frying your yum yums, it's important to have the oil very hot so that they become crispy and golden-brown on the outside – use a sugar thermometer to slowly bring it to a temperature of 170-180°C. And be very careful while cooking with hot oil! Add the yum yums to the pan gently so that oil doesn't spatter, and never leave the pan unattended.

Yum yums

Yum yums are a twist on doughnuts – because ye twist the dough intae twirls! It can take a wee while tae make them because ye hae tae leave the dough tae prove, but they're weel worth the effort. After ye've glazed them wi' sugar and left them tae set, they're, well, yum yum!

Frying pan
Cling film
Rolling pin
Pastry brush

For the dough:
500g strong bread flour
15g dried yeast
Pinch of salt
1 tablespoon sugar
50g unsalted butter
1 egg
250ml water
Oil for frying

For the glacé icing:
250g icing sugar
4 tablespoons water

1. In a large bowl add flour, yeast, salt, sugar and butter and rub together until large breadcrumbs are formed – don't overwork mixture

2. Add egg and water and mix together tae form a soft dough

3. Cover dough in the bowl and cover wi' cling film, then set aside tae prove for 1 hour

4. Once the dough has increased in size, roll intae a rectangle

5. Wi' the narrow side facing ye, fold both narrow ends intae the centre then fold in half

6. Make a half turn and fold in half again

7. Roll oot the dough and repeat the folding process once more

8. Leave dough tae prove for 2 hours

9. On a lightly floured surface, roll oot dough intae a rectangle shape approximately 5mm thick

10. Cut intae strips approximately 1½" by 4"

11. Cut a slit in the centre of each strip, being careful not tae cut in half

12. Twist the strip intae a twisted yum yum shape

13. In a bowl, add a' the icing sugar and mix in a little water at a time until mixture is very runny with no lumps, tae make glacé icing

14. Fry the yum yums in hot oil for around 2 tae 3 minutes on each side or until golden-brown

15. Brush wi' the glacé icing mix while still hot then leave tae set

Cheese twists

The combination o' flaky, buttery pastry and sharp, tangy cheese makes mah cheese twists a finger-lickin' crunchy delight. Using different cheeses adds a bit o' variety – try your own mixes! Serve them in a newspaper cone if ye want tae make them look a bit fancy. That's whit I dae – once Granpaw's finished readin' 'The Post'!

Baking tray

Baking paper

Measuring jug

Rolling pin

Pastry brush

1 medium egg

1 tablespoon water

1x flaky pastry recipe

250g Parmesan and mozzarella cheese, grated and mixed

1 medium egg, beaten, tae glaze

1. Preheat non-fan oven tae 200°C

2. Line a baking tray with baking paper

3. Whisk egg and water together in a measuring jug

4. Roll oot pastry intae a square shape tae approximately 3mm thick

5. Brush surface of pastry wi' the egg wash

6. Sprinkle half the cheese on half of the pastry and fold over

7. Seal edges gently with a pinch

8. Brush the top of your pastry wi' egg wash and cover with remaining cheese

9. Cut intae narrow strips

10. Twist strips intae spirals and place on prepared baking tray

11. Bake in the centre of the oven for 10 minutes or until golden-brown

95

Scotch pies

This is Scotland's favourite pie, and it's the Broon menfolk's favourite too! Paw, Granpaw, Hen and Joe might bite intae them while they're at the fitba, but they a' agree that mah home-made ones are the best.

MAKES SIX
Large glass jug
4" round pastry cutter
6" round pastry cutter
Six 4" baking rings
Baking tray
Greaseproof paper
Pastry brush

For the pastry:
225g dripping
300ml boiling water
680g self-raising flour
1 teaspoon salt
A little milk, tae glaze

For the filling:
500g minced lamb
225g breadcrumbs
Salt and pepper, tae season

1. In a large glass jug, add the dripping and carefully pour in the boiling water

2. Mix carefully until dripping has melted

3. In a large bowl, sift the flour and salt and make a well in the middle

4. Pour in the dripping and water mix, and stir wi' a wooden spoon until a dough forms

5. Leave until cool enough tae handle and knead wi' your hands until smooth and elastic

6. Place back in the bowl and cover the bowl wi' a clean tea towel

7. Leave tae rest in a warm place until firmer tae the touch

8. Roll oot pastry tae approximately 3-4mm thick

9. Cut six pastry cases with a 6" round cutter and six lids wi' a 4" round cutter

10. Place six 4" baking rings on a lined baking tray

11. Very gently line each ring wi' pastry and set aside

12. Preheat non-fan oven tae 190°C

13. In a large bowl, thoroughly mix the minced lamb, breadcrumbs and seasoning

14. Fill each case three-quarters full and place a pastry lid on top, then seal around edge wi' a little water and pinch gently

15. Cut a small hole in the centre of each lid, tae allow steam tae escape

16. Brush wi' a little milk

17. Place in the oven for 25 minutes or until golden-brown

Forfar bridies

Traditionally, Forfar bridies are made with shortcrust pastry, but throughout the rest of Scotland flaky pastry is used, and it's mah preference too. A bridie is a bit like a Cornish pastie, but because it just has mince and nae tatties it's a bit lighter. It makes a braw filling lunch and is a firm favourite wi' oor strapping lad Joe.

MAKES SIX

Large bowl
Rolling pin
Baking tray

1x flaky pastry recipe
700g lean minced beef
1 onion, finely chopped
60g unsalted butter
60ml beef stock
1 teaspoon mustard powder
Salt and pepper, tae season

1. Preheat non-fan oven tae 230°C

2. In a large bowl, add the minced beef, onion, butter, stock, mustard powder and seasoning. Mix well

3. Split pastry intae 6 equal amounts

4. On a lightly floured surface, roll oot each piece in a circle approximately ½" thick and 6" in diameter

5. Divide the prepared filling intae six and spoon onto the centre of each of the pastry pieces

6. Leave a 1" edge uncovered and dampen wi' a little water

7. Fold over the pastry and seal edges securely with a pinch

8. Make 2 holes in the top of the pastry, tae allow steam tae escape

9. Place the bridies onto a lightly oiled baking tray

10. Bake in the centre of the oven for 15 minutes or until golden-brown

8.

Maw's Top Tips

Some braw Scottish pies are made wi' hot-water-crust pastry, which is fine and sturdy for holding robust fillings, like the minced lamb in mah Scotch pies or macaroni cheese in mah macaroni pies. Unlike other kinds o' pastry, which ye usually need tae keep cauld and handle as little as possible, this is made wi' hot water and dripping, and ye can handle it as much as ye like.

Macaroni pies

With crispy pastry filled with soft, cheesy pasta, macaroni pies are another Scottish speciality and great tae eat on the go. They might be stodgy, but they're delicious too. Enjoy with some brown or HP sauce on top. Braw!

MAKES SIX
Large glass jug
Rolling pin
4" round pastry cutter
6" round pastry cutter
Six 4" round baking rings
Greaseproof paper
Large saucepan

For the pastry:
225g dripping
300ml boiling water
680g self-raising flour
1 teaspoon salt

For the filling:
450g dried macaroni
180g unsalted butter
180g plain flour
250ml milk
3 teaspoons English mustard
200g Cheddar cheese, grated
Salt and pepper, tae season

1. Add the dripping tae a large glass jug and carefully pour in the boiling water

2. Mix carefully until dripping has melted

3. In a large bowl, sift the flour and salt and make a well in the middle

4. Pour in the dripping and water mix, and stir wi' a wooden spoon until a dough forms

5. Leave until cool enough tae handle and knead wi' your hands until smooth and elastic

6. Place back in the bowl and cover the bowl wi' a clean tea towel

7. Leave tae rest in a warm place until firmer tae touch

8. Roll oot pastry quite thin – approximately 3-4mm thick

9. Cut six pastry cases with a 6" round cutter and six lids wi' a 4" round cutter

10. Place six 4" baking rings on a lined baking tray

11. Very gently line each ring with pastry and set aside

12. Preheat non-fan oven tae 190°C

13. Cook macaroni in a pot of salted boiling water for approximately 10 tae 12 minutes or until almost cooked

14. Drain macaroni and set aside

15. In a saucepan, melt the butter on a low heat and add the flour, stirring constantly

16. Once a' the flour is incorporated, add the mustard and mix

17. Add the milk a little at a time until a smooth paste forms. Use a' the milk

18. Add three-quarters of the grated cheese and season tae taste

19. Add the macaroni tae the sauce and very gently mix

20. Spoon mixture intae pasty cases and sprinkle wi' remaining grated cheese

21. Bake in preheated oven for 12 tae 15 minutes

22. Cool in rings

Mince pies

Mince pies are a must at Christmastime. Crumbly pastry and fruity, nutty mincemeat make for a true taste of Christmas. If you're feeling indulgent, why not try them wi' some brandy butter?

MAKES 12
12-well tart tin
Rolling pin
Pastry brush

For the bases and lids:
1x sweet pastry recipe

For the mincemeat:
250g raisins
350g currants
Zest and juice of one lemon
50ml brandy
300g shredded suet
250g dark brown sugar
1 large bramley apple, peeled, cored and chopped
100g mixed peel, chopped
1 teaspoon nutmeg
1 medium egg, beaten, tae glaze
Icing sugar, tae dust

1. Soak the raisins and currants in the lemon juice and brandy for 1 hour

2. Add the rest of the ingredients (except the egg and icing sugar) and mix well

3. Preheat non-fan oven tae 200°C

4. Take a tablespoon of pastry and press intae the well of a tart tin, lining the sides and bottom

5. Repeat until a' 12 wells are lined

6. Fill each case with a spoon of mincemeat, not more than $^3/_4$ full

7. Roll oot remaining pastry and cut lids tae fit a' 12 pies

8. Place lids onto the pies and seal around the edges by pinching wi' thumb and forefinger

9. Brush the lids wi' a little beaten egg

10. Bake in the preheated oven for 20 minutes or until golden-brown

11. Remove from oven and cool in the tin

12. Remove from tin and dust with icing sugar

Tip

Eat warm with custard cream or even ice cream

5

Biscuits

Simple shortbread

Shortbread is one o' those recipes that looks so simple but is easy tae get wrong. If ye want soft, melting shortbread, it needs slow, careful baking. I use icing sugar in the mix tae get the perfect texture but sprinkle caster sugar on the top for crunch. Horace always has a piece when he's daein' his homework tae gie him a boost, and it's always a Broons favourite, no matter whit they're a' daein'.

2 baking trays
Baking paper
Rolling pin
2" round cookie cutter

300g plain flour
60g icing sugar
250g unsalted butter, cold, cubed
Caster sugar, tae sprinkle

1. Preheat non-fan oven tae 150°C

2. Grease and line two baking trays

3. Sift flour and icing sugar together in a large mixing bowl

4. Rub butter intae flour and sugar until it reaches breadcrumb consistency

5. Knead mixture in the bowl until it combines tae make a smooth dough

6. Roll oot dough to 5mm thickness and cut into circles with 2" round cutter

7. Place biscuits on prepared baking trays, spaced well apart

8. Bake in preheated oven for 15 tae 20 minutes or until golden-brown

9. Sprinkle wi' caster sugar

10. Cool in tin before transferring tae a wire rack and cooling completely

Luxury shortbread

Mah simple shortbread is delicious, but I call this recipe mah luxury shortbread. Semolina might not sound very luxurious, but adding it in gives the shortbread an even more crumbly, melting texture.

Two baking trays
Baking paper
Rolling pin
Round cookie cutter

225g unsalted butter
120g granulated sugar
280g plain flour
60g semolina
Caster sugar, tae sprinkle

1. Line two baking trays wi' baking paper
2. Cream butter and sugar until light and fluffy
3. Stir in flour and semolina
4. Roll oot on a lightly floured surface tae approximately 1cm thickness
5. Using a round cookie cutter, cut dough intae circles and place on prepared baking trays, spaced well apart
6. Place both trays in the fridge tae chill for 1 hour
7. Preheat non-fan oven tae 160°C
8. Bake in preheated oven for 30 minutes or until golden-brown
9. Cool completely on a wire rack
10. Sprinkle with caster sugar

Caramel shortbread

Caramel shortbread goes by many names: millionaire's shortbread, caramel shortcake... but whatever ye call it, it cannae be denied that crumbly shortbread, oozy caramel and thick chocolate is a winning combination. The family always make short work of this whenever I make a batch!

Swiss roll tray
Baking paper
Saucepan
Heatproof bowl

For the shortbread:
250g plain flour
75g caster sugar
175g unsalted butter, softened

For the caramel:
100g unsalted butter
100g light muscovado sugar
2x 397g tins of condensed milk

For the topping:
200g dark chocolate, broken intae pieces

1. Preheat non-fan oven tae 180°C

2. Grease and line Swiss roll tray

3. In a large bowl, mix the flour and sugar

4. Add the butter and rub in tae form breadcrumbs

5. Knead mixture tae form a dough

6. Press the dough intae the prepared tray and level

7. Prick the dough thoroughly wi' a fork

8. Bake in the preheated oven for 20 minutes or until golden-brown

9. Remove from oven and allow tae cool in the tin

10. In a saucepan, add the butter, sugar and condensed milk and heat gently until a' the sugar is dissolved

11. Bring the mixture tae the boil before reducing the heat and simmering for around 5 minutes or until the mixture thickens and then allow to cool for 10 tae 15 minutes

12. Pour the sauce over the shortbread base and allow tae cool and set

13. Melt the chocolate in a heatproof bowl over a saucepan of gently simmering water

14. Pour the chocolate over the caramel layer and place in the fridge tae set

Tip

Allow the chocolate tae cool a little, then score the top intae the size tae be cut: this will allow easier cutting once set

Empire biscuits

Whenever mah cronies come roond for afternoon tea and a guid gossip, I always make sure tae hae a batch o' mah empire biscuits on the table. They're basically two shortbread biscuits sandwiched together wi' jam, but the icing and cherry on the top make them just that wee bit more special.

Baking tray

Baking paper

Rolling pin

Round cookie cutter

For the biscuits:

225g unsalted butter

85g icing sugar

320g plain flour

Mixed fruit jam, tae sandwich biscuits together

For the topping:

225g icing sugar

Glacé cherries or fruit jellies

1. Preheat non-fan oven tae 160°C

2. Grease and line baking tray

3. Cream the butter and sugar until light and fluffy

4. Mix in the flour tae form a soft dough

5. On a floured surface, roll oot the dough tae 5mm thickness

6. Using a round cookie cutter, cut circles in the size of your choice

7. Place onto prepared baking tray

8. Bake in the oven for 15 tae 20 minutes or until golden-brown

9. Cool on wire rack

10. Once cool, sandwich two biscuits together wi' a teaspoon of jam and set aside on a wire rack

11. For the topping, mix the icing sugar wi' a little water until runny tae make glacé icing

12. Swirl icing over each biscuit, allowing it tae run over edges

13. Finish off by placing a glacé cherry or small fruit jelly on top

109

9.
Maw's Top Tips

Ye might want tae eat this giant empire biscuit as soon
as ye can, but make sure ye cool the two halves in the tins
before removing. If the biscuit is still hot and slightly
soft, it could break apart while you're taking it out.
I promise ye, it'll be worth the wait!

Giant empire biscuit

For something spectacular, why not try mah giant empire biscuit? It's just the same recipe as mah empire biscuits, only bigger and maybe even better! It makes a braw centrepiece for afternoon tea. Your friends will be fallin' ower each other tae grab a slice!

Two 8" round cake tins
Baking paper

For the biscuits:
225g unsalted butter
85g icing sugar
320g plain flour
Mixed fruit jam, tae sandwich biscuits together

For the topping:
225g icing sugar
Glacé cherries or fruit jellies

1. Preheat non-fan oven tae 160°C

2. Grease and line two 8" round cake tins

3. Cream the butter and sugar until light and fluffy

4. Mix in the flour tae form a soft dough

5. Split the mixture intae the two prepared cake tins

6. Bake in the oven for 30 minutes or until golden-brown

7. Cool on wire rack

8. Once cool, sandwich the two biscuits together wi' the jam and set aside on a wire rack

9. For the topping, mix the icing sugar wi' a little water until runny tae make glacé icing

10. Swirl icing over the biscuit, allowing it tae run over edges

11. Finish off by placing a glacé cherry or small fruit jelly on top

Chocolate-chip cookie surprise

On the odd occasion the Twins are guid wee laddies, I gie them a special treat: mah chocolate-chip cookie surprise! They look like chocolate-chip cookies from the outside, but when ye bite intae them – well, ye'll just hae tae bake them yourself and see. The look on the Twins' faces is priceless! And if ye bake them yourself, they're always good value!

Two baking trays
Baking paper

150g salted butter
80g caster sugar
80g light muscovado sugar
1 large egg
2 teaspoons vanilla extract
225g plain flour
½ teaspoon bicarbonate of soda
Pinch of salt
200g milk chocolate drops
'Surprises' of your choice. I use Oreo or jam-sandwich biscuits, or any bite-size treat

1. Preheat non-fan oven tae 190°C
2. Grease and line two baking trays
3. Cream the butter and sugars together until light and fluffy
4. Add the egg and vanilla. Beat well
5. Add the flour, bicarbonate of soda and salt. Mix well
6. Add the chocolate chips and mix
7. Split mixture intae two halves and, using a teaspoon, use one half of the mixture tae dollop individual biscuit onto the prepared trays, spacing well apart
8. Press a 'surprise' intae each biscuit
9. Spoon the remaining half of the mixture on top of each surprise and gently flatten wi' your fingers, taking care tae press the edges and secure your surprise inside
10. Bake cookies in the oven for 12 tae 15 minutes or until golden-brown
11. Leave tae cool on the tray for a few minutes, then transfer tae a wire rack tae cool completely

113

Melting moments

Melting moments are just as soothing as they sound: beautiful melt-in-the-mouth biscuits wi' just a hint of vanilla. These are perfect at the end of the day when ye sit down in your armchair with a cup of tea and put your feet up. Ah!

Two large baking trays
Baking paper
Piping bag with star nozzle

350g unsalted butter
85g icing sugar
½ teaspoon vanilla extract
300g plain flour
50g cornflour

1. Preheat non-fan oven tae 180°C

2. Line two large baking trays with baking paper

3. Beat butter and sugar in a large bowl until light and fluffy

4. Add vanilla extract

5. Sift flour and cornflour over mixture and mix thoroughly

6. Using a piping bag wi' a star nozzle, pipe cookie swirls onto lined trays, spacing well apart

7. Bake in preheated oven for 15 tae 20 minutes

8. Cool on baking tray then transfer tae wire rack

SCOOP!

Viennese fingers

Viennese fingers are a sophisticated treat for tea parties. The buttery, crumbly biscuit is lovely on its own, but when ye bite intae the end that's been dipped in chocolate it takes it up another notch! It's nae surprise that they always disappear quickly in oor hoose.

Two large baking trays
Baking paper
Piping bag with a large star nozzle
Heatproof glass bowl
Saucepan

100g unsalted butter, softened
25g golden caster sugar
½ teaspoon vanilla extract
100g self-raising flour
100g dark chocolate, broken intae pieces

1. Preheat non-fan oven tae 160°C

2. Line two large baking trays with greaseproof paper

3. Beat butter, sugar and vanilla until light and fluffy

4. Stir in flour until mixture combines; it should look like a stiff dough

5. Using a piping bag with a large star nozzle, pipe fingers (approx. 2" long) onto lined trays, spaced well apart

6. Bake in preheated oven for 10 tae 15 minutes or until golden-brown

7. Leave on baking tray tae cool for 5 minutes before transferring tae a wire rack tae cool completely

8. Melt chocolate in a glass bowl over a saucepan of simmering water

9. Dip each end of the biscuit intae the chocolate and place on a sheet of baking paper tae set completely

Flapjacks

When Joe goes explorin' he always takes a tubful of mah flapjacks wi' him. Packed full o' oats and nuts, they're great for keepin' him goin'. And great for sharing wi' a cup o' tea!

8" square cake tin

Baking paper

Saucepan

200g rolled oats

115g hazelnuts, chopped

55g plain flour

115g unsalted butter

2 tablespoons golden syrup

85g light muscovado sugar

1. Preheat non-fan oven tae 180°C

2. Grease and line an 8" square cake tin

3. Mix the oats, hazelnuts and flour together in a large mixing bowl

4. Place the butter, syrup and sugar in a saucepan and stir together over a low heat until melted

5. Pour the butter, syrup and sugar mixture over the dry ingredients and mix together

6. Spoon the mixture intae the prepared cake tin and level the top

7. Bake in preheated oven for 20 tae 25 minutes or until golden-brown and firm tae touch

8. While still warm, score the top o' the flapjacks intae squares

9. Cool on a wire rack

10. Cut intae squares

10.
Maw's Top Tips

When cooking any kind o' biscuit, always make sure they're spaced well apart on the tray. This is because the mixture can melt and spread from the heat of the oven. So leaving plenty of space means when ye bring them out of the oven you'll have lots of individual biscuits – not just one giant biscuit!

Cheese biscuits

If ye ever have a hankering for cheese and biscuits, why not put the two together and gie mah cheese biscuits a try? Sweet biscuits are braw, but sometimes ye just cannae beat something savoury, and these tasty wee morsels are delicious.

Baking tray
Baking paper
Cling film
Rolling pin
1½" round pastry cutter

150g plain flour
150g Cheddar cheese, grated
150g unsalted butter, cubed
1 egg yolk

1. In a large bowl, add the flour and cheese and mix together

2. Add butter and rub in until crumbs form

3. Add egg yolk and knead together until a smooth dough is formed

4. Wrap mixture tightly in cling film and place in the fridge for at least 1 hour tae cool

5. Preheat non-fan oven tae 200°C

6. Line a baking tray wi' a sheet of baking paper

7. Remove from the fridge and leave for 10 minutes before rolling oot on a lightly floured surface

8. Cut biscuits using a 1½" round pastry cutter and place on prepared tray

9. Bake on the oven for 10 minutes or until golden-brown

Tip

Substitute half of the flour with wholemeal plain flour for a wholesome alternative biscuit

6

Bread

White farmhouse loaf

It's well worth mastering this basic bread recipe: once ye do, the possibilities are endless. Nobody can resist the smell of freshly baked bread so be prepared for gannets tearing intae it as soon as it's oot the oven!

2lb loaf tin
Large bowl
Cling film

450g strong white flour
1½ teaspoons dried yeast
1 teaspoon salt
1 teaspoon granulated sugar
300ml lukewarm water
1 tablespoon olive oil

Tips

When it's ready bread sounds hollow when tapped

Split the dough intae smaller-sized balls and bake on a baking tray tae make morning rolls, or make golf-ball-sized balls, top with seeds and serve with soup or as a dinner roll

1. Preheat non-fan oven tae 220°C

2. Oil and flour a 2lb loaf tin

3. In a large bowl, mix the flour, yeast, salt and sugar together

4. Make a well in the centre of the dry ingredients and pour in the water and oil

5. Mix wi' hands tae form soft dough

6. Add a little extra water if required

7. Knead the dough on a lightly floured surface for around 10 minutes or until smooth and elastic

8. Form the dough intae a ball and place in an oiled bowl, smooth side up, and cover with cling film. Leave in a warm place for at least 1 hour or until doubled in size

9. Gently knead the dough and form intae a rectangle shape tae fit prepared tin

10. Place dough intae tin and cover loosely wi' cling film

11. Leave tae rise for a further 30 minutes

12. Dust the top wi' a little flour

13. Bake in the oven for 20 minutes

14. Reduce temperature tae 200°C and bake for a further 20 minutes or until golden-brown

15. Turn oot loaf onto a wire rack and cool

Easy oatmeal bread

Oatmeal bread is rich, nutty and chewy, and a braw way tae get more fibre in your diet, making it better for ye than a normal white loaf. It's handy for using up leftover oats, too.

Baking tray
Food processor
Measuring jug

75g porridge oats
100g wholemeal flour
10g baking powder
Pinch of salt
1 tablespoon local honey
1 tablespoon olive oil
215ml skimmed milk

1. Preheat non-fan oven tae 230°C

2. Lightly oil a baking tray

3. Place the oats in a food processor and grind

4. In a large bowl add flour, oats, baking powder and salt and gie a quick mix

5. In a measuring jug, add the honey and oil and stir in milk

6. Make a well in the dry ingredients and pour in the milk mixture

7. Mix together tae form a soft dough

8. Gently form the dough intae a loaf shape and place on prepared baking tray

9. Bake in the centre of the oven for 20 minutes or until golden-brown

10. Cool on a wire rack or eat hot

Wholemeal loaf

Mah wholemeal loaf is packed full o' the fibre and nutrients ye get from the whole grains, so it's better for ye than white bread. But more than that, it's delicious!

2lb loaf tin
Large bowl
Cling film
Pastry brush

225g strong white flour
225g strong wholemeal flour
1½ teaspoons dried yeast
1 teaspoon salt
150ml lukewarm water
1 tablespoon olive oil
200ml lukewarm milk
1 tablespoon local honey
1 medium egg, beaten, tae glaze

1. Preheat non-fan oven tae 220°C

2. Oil and flour a 2lb loaf tin

3. In a large bowl mix the flours, yeast and salt together

4. Make a well in the centre of the dry ingredients and pour in the water, oil, milk and honey

5. Mix wi' your hands tae form a soft, sticky dough

6. Place back in the bowl, cover with cling film and leave tae rest for 15 minutes

7. Knead the dough on a lightly floured surface for around 10 minutes or until soft and slightly springy

8. Form the dough intae a ball and place in an oiled bowl, smooth side up, and cover wi' cling film. Leave in a warm place for at least 1 hour or until doubled in size

9. Gently knead the dough and form intae a rectangle shape tae fit prepared tin

10. Place dough intae tin and cover loosely wi' cling film

11. Leave tae rise for a further 30 minutes

12. Brush wi' a little beaten egg and sprinkle some wholemeal flour on the top

13. Bake in the oven for 20 minutes

14. Reduce temperature tae 200°C and bake for a further 20 minutes

15. Turn oot loaf onto a wire rack and cool

125

Dinner rolls

These easy-tae-bake rolls make a wonderful accompaniment tae dinner. The seeds on top add crunch – choose your favourite!

Baking tray
Large bowl
Cling film
Pastry brush

225g strong white flour
225g strong wholemeal flour
1½ teaspoons dried yeast
1 teaspoon salt
150ml lukewarm water
1 tablespoon olive oil
200ml lukewarm milk
1 tablespoon local honey
1 medium egg, beaten, tae glaze
**Variety of seeds of your choice
– sesame, pumpkin, poppy etc.,
tae sprinkle**

1. Preheat non-fan oven tae 220°C

2. Oil and flour a baking tray

3. In a large bowl mix the flours, yeast and salt together

4. Make a well in the centre of the dry ingredients and pour in the water, oil, milk and honey

5. Mix wi' hands tae form a soft, sticky dough

6. Place back in the bowl, cover wi' cling film and leave tae rest for 15 minutes

7. Knead the dough on a lightly floured surface for around 10 minutes or until soft and slightly springy

8. Form the dough intae a ball and place in an oiled bowl, smooth side up, and cover wi' cling film. Leave in a warm place for at least 1 hour or until doubled in size

9. Gently knead the dough and split intae small balls

10. Place dough balls onto baking tray and cover loosely wi' cling film

11. Leave tae rise for a further 30 minutes

12. Brush each ball wi' a little beaten egg and sprinkle some seeds on the top

13. Bake in the oven for 20 minutes

14. Reduce temperature tae 200°C and bake for a further 20 minutes

15. Turn oot rolls onto a wire rack and cool

Sweet morning rolls

Mah sweet morning rolls are the Scottish equivalent of brioche: bread that's enriched wi' sugar and eggs tae gie a moist, slightly sweet crumb. Enjoy these rolls as part o' a special breakfast, perhaps wi' smoked salmon and scrambled eggs.

12-hole muffin tray
Large bowl
Cling film

375g strong white flour
50g caster sugar
7g dried yeast
2 teaspoons salt
100ml warm milk
3 medium eggs
175g unsalted butter
1 medium egg, beaten, tae glaze

1. In a large bowl, mix the flour, sugar, yeast and salt

2. Add the milk and 3 eggs and mix tae form a dough

3. Knead in the bowl for 10 minutes

4. Add the butter tae the dough and knead for a further 10 minutes

5. Place the dough in a lightly oiled bowl, cover wi' cling film and place in the fridge overnight

6. Grease a 12-hole muffin tray and divide dough intae 12 equal pieces

7. Gently roll each piece intae a ball and place intae the tin

8. Loosely cover the tray wi' cling film and set aside for 1 hour

9. Preheat non-fan oven tae 190°C

10. Glaze the top o' each roll with the remaining beaten egg

11. Bake in the centre o' the oven for 10 tae 12 minutes or until golden-brown

12. Cool on a wire rack

Drop scones/Scotch pancakes

Whether ye call them drop scones or Scotch pancakes, these are a staple of any Scottish baker! They're very versatile: they can be eaten hot or cold, smothered in golden syrup for dessert, or spread wi' butter and jam as part of an afternoon tea. But the best time of a' tae eat them is, of course, on Pancake Day.

Baking tray
Frying pan
Pallet knife
Tea towel

225g plain flour
4 teaspoons baking powder
1 large egg
2 teaspoons golden syrup
200ml milk
Oil for frying

1. Fold a clean tea towel in half and place on a baking tray

2. Intae a large bowl, sift the flour and baking powder

3. Make a well in the centre and add the egg, syrup and milk

4. Whisk until mixture is smooth and lump-free

5. Place a little oil in a frying pan, just enough tae coat the pan, and heat

6. Gently pour a little batter intae pan and spread tae desired size by carefully tilting the pan in a circular motion

7. Once bubbles start tae appear on the surface of the pancake, flip over wi' a pallet knife and cook on the other side until golden-brown

8. Once cooked, remove from the pan and place inside your folded tea towel

9. Repeat process until a' the batter is used, remembering tae lightly oil the pan each time

10. Best served warm wi' one of the following: butter, golden syrup, freshly squeezed lemon juice, fresh fruit and cream

11.
Maw's Top Tips

It's the air bubbles that make crumpets special. Tae make sure ye get plenty, leave the mix alone for the full two hours: this gives the bubbles time tae develop. And when it comes time tae cook them, dinnae flip them over too early: wait until the top loses that wet look and is covered wi' bubbles.

Crumpets

Crumpets are similar tae pancakes but are thicker and have a unique spongy texture that's ideal for soaking up lashings o' butter. Best served warm, straight from the griddle, these are a homely, comforting treat.

4 crumpet or muffin rings
Frying pan

125g plain flour
125g strong white flour
½ teaspoon dried yeast
175ml tepid milk
175ml tepid water
½ teaspoon salt
½ teaspoon bicarbonate of soda
2 tablespoons tepid water
Oil for frying

1. In a large bowl, mix flours and yeast
2. Make a well in the centre of the flour mixture, pour in the milk and water, and mix well
3. Leave for 2 hours: bubbles will rise then fall
4. In a separate bowl, mix the salt and bicarbonate of soda wi' 2 tablespoons of tepid water
5. Add this tae the flour mixture and whisk
6. Leave the mixture tae rest for 5 minutes
7. Oil 4 crumpet rings
8. Place the rings onto a lightly oiled frying pan and place over a medium heat
9. Pour batter intae each ring tae a height of approximately 1½ cm
10. Cook for 8 minutes or until batter is firm tae touch and the surface is covered in air bubbles
11. Remove rings and flip crumpet over
12. Cook for a further 2 minutes or until golden-brown
13. Serve warm wi' butter or toast tae reheat

Selkirk bannock

Bannocks are a braw traditional Scottish bread cooked on a griddle. There are lots o' different regional variations on bannocks, but this simple recipe is Paw's favourite. He likes nothin' better than sittin' back in his armchair wi' a freshly baked slice spread wi' butter.

7" round cake tin
Large bowl
Cling film
Saucepan
Pastry brush

450g strong plain white flour
7g dried yeast
115g caster sugar
150ml milk
120g unsalted butter
225g sultanas
60g mixed peel
A little milk, tae glaze

1. In a large bowl, add the flour, yeast and sugar. Mix well

2. In a saucepan, add the milk and butter, and melt over a low heat

3. Make a well in the flour and pour in the milk and butter mixture

4. Mix well tae form a smooth dough

5. Leave in the bowl and loosely cover wi' cling film, then leave in a warm place tae rest for 1 hour

6. Knead the dough well for a few minutes in the bowl

7. Add the sultanas and mixed peel and continue tae knead

8. Preheat non-fan oven tae 180°C

9. Oil a 7" round cake tin

10. Place the dough in the tin and loosely cover wi' cling film, then leave tae prove for 30 minutes

11. Remove the cling film and bake the dough in the centre of a preheated oven for 1 hour

12. Brush the top of the bannock wi' a little milk and return tae the oven for a further 20 minutes

13. Cool in the tin before transferring tae a wire rack tae cool completely

Tip

Beware – stirring bannocks anticlockwise was traditionally thought tae be bad luck!

PEACE AT LAST !

Tattie scones

Tattie scones are a breakfast favourite wi' oor family. Shop-bought are fine but home-made are something special. The secret is tae use a guid floury potato that'll go fluffy and soft, which will gie your tattie scones a perfect texture. Serve as part o' a traditional Scottish breakfast.

3" cookie cutter
Rolling pin
Heavy-bottomed frying pan

240g hot mashed potato
50g unsalted butter, melted
Salt and pepper, tae season
70g plain flour
Oil for frying

1. While the mashed potato is still hot, add the butter and season tae taste

2. Add the flour tae the potato a little at a time and mix tae form a soft dough

3. On a lightly floured surface, roll the dough tae approximately ½" thick

4. Using a cookie cutter, cut 3" circles until a' the dough is used

5. Prick each tattie scone a' over the surface wi' a fork

6. In a heavy-bottomed frying pan, add a little oil and heat

7. Fry each scone for 2 tae 3 minutes on each side until golden-brown

7
Sweets
and
Treats

12.
Maw's Top Tips

When making sweets like tablet, fudge and toffee, it's important tae get the mixture tae the right temperature. Using a sugar thermometer is the most reliable way tae get the best results, but ye can also use the 'cold water' test to check if your mixture has achieved the right consistency. Just drop a little of the mixture intae a glass of very cold water, leave for a minute or so, then pick it up and roll it between your finger and thumb tae see how it feels. For the recipes in this book, these are the stages you're looking for:

Fudge: The temperature should be 115°C or when using the cold water test should reach the 'soft ball' stage, where it forms a – surprise! – soft ball that flattens instantly when ye rub it between your fingers.

Tablet: As above, the temperature should be 115°C or when using the cold water test should reach the 'soft ball' stage.

Toffee: temperature should be 160°C or should in the cold water test form a short thread of syrup that breaks sharply – this is known as the 'hard crack' stage.

Fudge

Fudge is similar tae tablet but has a softer texture because it's beaten for longer after it's cooked. It's another indulgent treat that ye can add just about anything tae: nuts, fruit, chocolate… the sky's the limit!

8" square tin
Baking paper
Small glass of cold water
Large non-stick saucepan

115g unsalted butter
450g soft brown sugar
397g tin of condensed milk
1 teaspoon vanilla extract
150ml milk

1. Grease and line an 8" square tin

2. In a large non-stick saucepan, gently heat the butter, sugar, condensed milk, vanilla extract and milk for around 15 minutes

3. Regularly scrape the bottom of the pan tae prevent the mixture from burning

4. The mixture is ready when a soft ball is formed when a spoonful is dropped intae a glass of cold water

5. Remove from heat and beat well wi' a wooden spoon for around 10 minutes or until the mixture has thickened considerably

6. Pour the mixture intae your prepared tin and allow tae cool completely

7. Remove from tin and cut intae squares

Tip

Substitute vanilla for any flavour of your choice for a twist

Alternatively, add 100g of chocolate chips, chopped nuts or dried fruit

Tablet

Now, they'll tell ye that sugary, buttery tablet isnae guid for ye, but I always say that a little bit o' whit ye fancy does ye guid! (Not too much, mind!) Mah tablet always used tae go missin' shortly after it was ready, but then I found Granpaw's secret stash in his drawer when I was puttin' his hankies awa' – whit a cheek! So it's back tae peppermints for him!

Swiss roll tray or baking tray with high edges
Large heavy-bottomed saucepan
Trivet or tea towel
Electric mixer (optional)

115g unsalted butter
1kg granulated sugar
130ml full fat milk
397g tin of condensed milk
1 teaspoon vanilla extract

1. Grease and line a Swiss roll tray

2. In a large heavy-bottomed saucepan add the butter, sugar and full fat milk and melt on the lowest heat setting

3. Simmer for approximately 1 hour or until the mixture has reached a rolling boil and plenty of bubbles are forming

4. Add the condensed milk and simmer until bubbles reform

5. Remove pan from the heat and place on a trivet or tea towel

6. Add vanilla and beat the mixture wi' a wooden spoon for around 20 minutes or wi' an electric mixer for around 5 minutes

7. Once the mixture has cooled considerably it will become very thick

8. Pour the mixture intae prepared tray and leave tae set completely

9. Cut intae squares

13.

Maw's Top Tips

Working with hot sugar can be dangerous as the temperatures rise very high and if spilled can cause bad burns. As a precaution, have cool (not ice-cold) water handy so you can plunge your hand into it if it gets burned. Never taste your mixture until it's cooled. And it goes withoot saying that bairns shouldn't be around when you're making these kinds of recipes.

Toffee

Toffee is sugary, sweet and sticky, and getting your teeth stuck together is a' part o' the fun. But the Twins' favourite bit is smashin' it tae bits wi' a toffee hammer when it's set!

Swiss roll tray or shallow baking tray
Sugar thermometer
Heavy-bottomed saucepan
Toffee hammer

125g unsalted butter
200g caster sugar
60ml water
Pinch of salt
1 teaspoon vanilla extract

1. Lightly grease a shallow baking tray or Swiss roll tray

2. In a large heavy-bottomed saucepan add butter, sugar, water and salt

3. Over a medium heat, cook the mixture, being careful tae stir continuously

4. Using a sugar thermometer, bring the mixture tae a temperature of 160°C

5. Remove pan from the heat and beat in the vanilla

6. Pour mixture intae prepared tray

7. Chill until completely set

8. Break intae pieces with a toffee hammer

143

Coconut ice

Mah coconut ice makes an exotic sugary treat on a summer's day. Coloured pink and cut intae dainty squares, it's pretty as a picture and a favourite o' oor Maggie while she's oot sunbathin'!

Deep 8" square cake tin
Cling film

330g desiccated coconut
350g icing sugar
397g tin of condensed milk
½ teaspoon vanilla extract
Red food colouring

1. Grease and line a deep 8" square cake tin

2. In a large bowl, mix together the coconut, icing sugar, condensed milk and vanilla

3. Spoon half the mixture intae the prepared cake tin and level wi' the back of a spoon

4. Add a few drops of red food colouring tae the remaining mixture and mix well

5. Spoon the pink mixture intae the tin, on top of the white layer, and level wi' the back of a spoon

6. Cover the tin wi' cling film and leave in a cool place tae set overnight

7. Once set, remove from tin and cut intae squares

145

14.

Maw's Top Tips

Chocolate can be temperamental, so handle it carefully. A foolproof way tae melt it is to put broken pieces in a heatproof bowl, then place the bowl over a saucepan of very gently simmering water, makin' sure that the base of the bowl doesn't touch the water itself – the chocolate can become grainy if it's overheated. Stir regularly until the chocolate melts and becomes smooth and glossy, then remove from the heat and use as directed.

Macaroon bars

Macaroon bars are a famous Scottish sweetie, and ye widnae believe the secret ingredient: a potato! It sounds a wee bit odd, but using cooled mashed potato gies a lovely, melting texture like fondant. Covered in chocolate and rolled in desiccated coconut, they're a treat like no other.

8" square tin
Heatproof bowl
Baking tray

1 small potato
500g icing sugar
200g dark chocolate, broken intae pieces
170g sweetened coconut

1. Grease and line an 8" square tin

2. Peel and dice potato and boil in a pan of boiling water for approximately 10 minutes or until cooked

3. Drain potato and mash tae remove a' lumps

4. In a large bowl, add two tablespoons o' mashed potato and add the icing sugar a little bit at a time. Mix well in between putting the sugar in. The mixture will be very stiff, and that's the right consistency. It'll build your muscles!

5. Pour mixture intae prepared tin and smooth down the top wi' the back of a spoon

6. Place in the fridge tae set

7. Once set, remove mixture from the tray and cut intae squares or bars

8. Return cut pieces tae the fridge while ye prepare the covering

9. Preheat non-fan oven tae 180°C

10. Place the broken chocolate pieces in a heatproof bowl and melt over a pan of gently simmering water

11. Place the sweetened coconut on a baking tray and place in the oven for a few minutes tae gently toast

12. Remove cut pieces from the fridge and dip intae the melted chocolate before covering in the toasted coconut

13. Return covered bars tae the fridge tae set completely

Peppermint creams

Peppermint creams are delicious minty fondants smothered in dark chocolate and they make a perfect wee mouthful. Daphne loves tae pop them intae her gob while she's gettin' ready tae go oot – well, if she ever stops yappin' long enough tae eat any!

Heatproof bowl
Baking tray
Baking paper
Small cookie cutter (use different shapes if ye like)

1 large egg, white only
1 teaspoon peppermint flavouring
Juice of ½ a lemon
420g icing sugar
175g dark chocolate, broken intae pieces

1. In a large bowl whisk the egg white until stiff peaks form

2. Whisk in peppermint and lemon juice

3. Add icing sugar a little at a time and mix well

4. On a surface dusted with icing sugar, roll oot the mixture tae 1cm thickness

5. Have fun cutting oot different shapes until a' the mixture is used

6. Slowly melt the chocolate in a heatproof bowl set over a saucepan of gently simmering water

7. Divide sweets intae 3 equal amounts

8. Dip ⅓ of the sweets completely in the chocolate and set aside on a baking tray covered wi' baking paper

9. Dip ⅓ of the sweets in chocolate, leaving half uncovered, and set aside on prepared baking tray

10. Drizzle the remaining chocolate over the remaining sweets and set aside on prepared baking tray

11. Place tray in the fridge for 60 minutes tae allow sweets tae set completely

Rocky road

Rocky road is a great way tae use up this and that: mah recipe uses digestive biscuits, marshmallows and walnuts, but ye could use anything sweet and crunchy ye have lying around. The name might say 'rocky', but it goes doon a treat.

8" square cake tin
Baking paper
Saucepan

125g unsalted butter
160g dark chocolate, broken intae pieces
160g milk chocolate, broken intae pieces
4 tablespoons golden syrup
100g digestive biscuits, broken intae pieces
100g mini marshmallows
100g walnuts, chopped

1. Grease and line an 8" square cake tin
2. In a saucepan, add butter, chocolate and golden syrup and melt over a low heat
3. Remove from heat and stir in remaining ingredients
4. Transfer mix tae the prepared tin
5. Chill in the fridge for 2 hours or until completely set
6. Remove from tin and cut intae squares

150

Puff candy

Whether ye call it honeycomb, puff candy or cinder toffee, it's always fun tae make this classic sweetie: wait till ye add the baking soda and see it erupt like a volcano! (Be careful, though, as it'll be hot as lava too!)

Baking tray
Baking paper
Saucepan

60g granulated sugar
2 tablespoons golden syrup
1 teaspoon bicarbonate of soda

1. Line a baking tray wi' baking paper

2. In a saucepan, add the sugar and golden syrup

3. Over a low heat, allow ingredients tae melt tae form a liquid, stirring continuously

4. Once melted, leave tae gently simmer until bubbles form. Do not stir

5. Once the mixture turns dark brown, remove from the heat

6. Add the bicarbonate of soda and whisk: the mixture will expand

7. Pour the mixture intae the prepared tray

8. Once set, break intae pieces

Simple chocolate truffles

There's nothing more delicious than mah melt-in-the-mouth chocolate truffles. Though ye normally see them wrapped up in posh boxes o' chocolates, they're surprisingly easy tae make yourself: gie them a go! I dare ye no' tae lick the spoon...

Two baking trays
Baking paper
Food processor
Heatproof bowl

300g Oreo biscuits
150g cream cheese
300g milk or dark chocolate, broken intae pieces

1. Line two baking trays wi' baking paper

2. Place the Oreo biscuits in a food processor and grind intae small crumbs

3. In a large bowl, add the cream cheese and a quarter of the biscuit crumbs and mix thoroughly

4. Continue tae add the biscuit crumbs until the mixture reaches a stiff consistency, keeping a little back for sprinkling over finished truffles

5. Take a teaspoon of mixture and roll intae a ball, then place onto prepared baking tray

6. Repeat until a' the mixture is used

7. Place the truffles intae the fridge tae chill for 1 hour

8. Melt the chocolate in a heatproof bowl over a saucepan of gently simmering water

9. Dip each truffle in the chocolate and carefully lift oot wi' a fork, giving the fork a quick tap on the side of the bowl tae remove any excess chocolate

10. Place covered truffles back onto the tray and sprinkle wi' the remaining biscuit crumbs before the chocolate sets

11. Return the trays tae the fridge for 30 minutes until the truffles have set completely

Tiffin

Tiffin is another one o' those recipes where ye can use up whatever bits and bobs ye hae lying around the kitchen. I use digestive biscuits and raisins in mine, a' bound together wi' syrup and chocolate. It disnae need bakin', so it's a guid one tae make wi' children an' they're a great wee present for any occasion!

8" square cake tin
Baking paper
Saucepan
Heatproof bowl

115g unsalted butter
30g caster sugar
2 tablespoons golden syrup
20g cocoa powder
225g rich tea biscuits, crushed
50g raisins
50g dried apricots, chopped
50g glacé cherries, chopped
120g dark chocolate
120g milk chocolate

1. Grease and line an 8" square cake tin

2. In a saucepan, melt the butter, sugar, golden syrup and cocoa powder

3. Remove from the heat and add the crushed biscuits, raisins, apricots and cherries

4. Press the mixture intae the prepared tin

5. Melt the chocolate in a heatproof bowl over a saucepan of gently simmering water

6. Pour the melted chocolate intae the tin

7. Place in the fridge tae set

8. Cut intae squares

Pecan brittle

Pecan brittle is so simple, but it's more than the sum o' its parts. It makes a satisfying crackle when ye break it intae bits and it's a crunchy treat for a' the family – especially if they're needin' some energy!

Baking tray

Large heavy-bottomed saucepan

Rolling pin

190g caster sugar

85g soft brown sugar

75ml water

25g unsalted butter

180g pecan nuts, broken intae pieces

½ teaspoon bicarbonate of soda

Pinch of salt

1. Grease a baking tray wi' a little oil

2. In a large heavy-bottomed saucepan, add the sugars and water

3. Stir over a medium heat until a' the sugar dissolves

4. Add the butter and stir until butter melts

5. Bring tae the boil and cook until golden-brown, stirring occasionally

6. Remove from the heat and add the pecan nuts, bicarbonate of soda and salt, and mix well

7. Pour onto the prepared tray and allow tae cool

8. Break intae pieces using a rolling pin

Donut sticks

These donut sticks are a fun twist on doughnuts. If ye cut them intae strips and serve them in a paper poke, they look just like chips! But instead o' salt, make sure ye sprinkle them wi' caster sugar or cinnamon sugar for added deliciousness. Just like bein' at the fair!

Deep frying pan
Rolling pin
Kitchen paper

250g self-raising flour
½ teaspoon baking powder
40g caster sugar
2 tablespoons milk
1 medium egg
150ml vegetable oil for frying
Caster sugar or ground cinnamon

1. In a large bowl add the flour, baking powder and sugar

2. Add the egg and one tablespoon of the oil and mix in the milk until a soft dough forms

3. On a lightly floured surface, roll oot the dough tae approximately 1cm thickness

4. Cut the dough intae thin strips

5. In a deep frying pan, heat the remaining oil

6. Place the strips intae the hot oil and fry on both sides until golden-brown and slightly crisp

7. Place the fried strips onto kitchen paper briefly, then roll in some caster sugar or a little ground cinnamon

8

Baking wi' Bairns

Mini sna' ba's

If ye thought mah cupcakes were cute, wait until ye see mah mini sna' ba's! Baked in a special 'cake pop' mould, these tiny coconut-dusted cakes are literally jam-packed with deliciousness! The Twins and the Bairn got hold of mah last batch saying they were going tae hae a 'sna' ba' fight', but I bet the lot will be snaffled in no time...

Cake-pop mould
Baking tray

For the sna' ba's:
60g unsalted butter
60g caster sugar
1 teaspoon vanilla
1 medium egg
120g self-raising flour
3 tablespoons milk

Tae decorate:
Strawberry jam
200g icing sugar
A little water
Desiccated coconut

1. Preheat non-fan oven tae 220°C

2. In a bowl, cream the butter, sugar and vanilla

3. Add egg and mix well

4. Alternate between adding flour and milk, mixing well

5. Spoon mixture intae cake-pop mould base and fill bottom completely

6. Place cake-pop mould lid on and bake on a baking tray in the centre of the oven for 10 tae 12 minutes

7. Leave cake balls tae cool in the mould

8. Cut each cake ball in half and fill the centre wi' a teaspoon of jam before reassembling

9. In a bowl, add the icing sugar and a teaspoon of water at a time, mixing until a thin, smooth glacé icing forms

10. Dip each ball intae the icing and lift oot wi' a fork, carefully tapping on the side of the bowl tae remove excess icing

11. Roll the ball in the coconut and set aside on a wire rack for a few hours tae dry completely

Mini iced gems

These cute little iced biscuits are the Bairn's absolute favourites. They're just the right size for her to serve to her dollies at tea parties – if the Bairn can stop herself munching away for long enough to share them oot! Use bright colours for the icing and they'll look like little gems – perfect for your wee treasures.

Two baking trays
Baking paper
Piping bag and star nozzle
Cling film
Round cookie cutter

For the biscuits:
200g plain flour
100g unsalted butter
100g caster sugar
1 medium egg
1 tablespoon golden syrup

Tae decorate:
2 medium eggs, whites only
500g icing sugar
4 different food colourings

1. Preheat non-fan oven tae 180°C

2. Line two baking trays wi' baking paper

3. In a large bowl add the flour, sugar and butter and rub in until mixture resembles breadcrumbs

4. Add the egg and syrup tae the mixture and combine ingredients tae form a soft dough

5. Cover dough wi' cling film and place in the fridge tae chill for half an hour

6. Place the dough between two pieces of baking paper and roll oot tae approximately 5mm

7. Using a small round cookie cutter or the wide end of a piping nozzle, cut oot biscuits and place on prepared trays

8. Bake in the centre of the oven for 6 tae 8 minutes

9. Cool completely on a wire rack

10. In a clean bowl, add egg whites and whisk by hand for 1 minute

11. Add a little of the icing sugar at a time and mix well until a thick consistency is reached and icing is smooth

12. Separate icing intae 4 bowls and colour each batch a different colour

13. Using a piping bag and small star nozzle, pipe a small rosette onto each biscuit and allow tae dry completely

Mini fruit tarts

These wee fruit tarts are colourful and cute and make perfect fruity mouthfuls for bairns. Just fill mini pastry tart cases with custard and then add your favourite fruit: I've used kiwi fruit, blueberries and strawberries, but experiment a' ye like!

Six mini tart tins

Baking paper

Baking beans or ceramic baking balls

For the base:
1x sweet pastry recipe

For the filling:
300ml custard
Selection of fruits – strawberries, raspberries, kiwi fruit, blackberries etc.
Icing sugar, tae dust

1. Preheat non-fan oven tae 180°C

2. Roll oot your pastry on a lightly floured surface

3. Carefully line six mini tart tins wi' the pastry and trim the excess

4. Place a small circle of baking paper on top of the pastry and fill wi' baking beans or ceramic baking balls

5. Place in the oven tae blind bake for approximately 15 minutes or until golden-brown

6. Allow the pastry tae cool completely

7. Fill each case wi' a generous amount of custard

8. Fill with the fruit and finish wi' a sprinkle of icing sugar

1. Make sweet pastry as per recipe and allow to rest for 10 minutes after removing from fridge

2. Roll oot the pastry on a floured surface

3. Gently press the pastry into a tart tin

4. Roll over the top of the tin to gie a sharp edge and remove any excess pastry

5. Line pastry wi' baking paper

6. Fill wi' baking beans

7. Bake in the oven as per recipe. Remove beans and paper and allow to cool in the tin

8. Fill the pastry case wi' a layer of custard (or cream if ye prefer)

9. Add fruit of your choice

10. Sprinkle with a little icing sugar

Handy tips for working wi' sugar paste

These days I normally buy sugar paste, ready tae use. Wi' a busy household, it makes life easier. There's a recipe on p186 if ye have time tae make it.

It takes a lot o' practice tae get used tae sugar paste, but it's really worth it in the end. Using sugar paste is a braw and clean alternative tae mixing icing – and ye won't get any crumbs in your mix! Here are a few wee tips I learned the hard way:

1. Ye need tae knead sugar paste till it's soft and pliable. If ye dinnae, it won't ever do what ye want it tae. Your warm hands will soften it easily.

2. Always make sure tae dust your surface very well wi' a lot o' icing sugar tae stop the paste from sticking.

3. If ye find that you're getting bubbles when you're rolling oot the paste, burst them immediately. Poke the bubble wi' a sterile needle or a cocktail stick and then roll the air oot o' the paste.

4. If you're mixing your own colours intae the paste, make sure that ye put the colourant in using a small amount on the tip o' a cocktail stick. They are awfy concentrated and if you're too heavy-handed wi' them then ye might end up wi' a colour that requires sunglasses! Leave it tae develop for 10 minutes after mixing before ye add more, because it turns darker.

5. Airtight freezer bags are braw for storing sugar paste and it doesn't need tae be in the fridge. The bags will stop the paste crusting over. The paste will be all right tae use for a couple o' weeks.

9

Gettin' Fancy

Paw Broon face cake

Whit better way tae show Paw we love him than by putting his face on a cake? We gave this tae Paw for his birthday and he loved it – the only thing was he didnae want us tae eat it! It might look complicated, but just follow mah step-by-step guide tae making your ain Paw cake.

Small brush
Knife
Pizza cutter
Small piece of tinfoil
Paw's face template

8" round cake covered wi' sugar paste
Flesh-coloured sugar paste
Dark-brown sugar paste
Dark-silver lustre dust
Lemon juice
Food glue
White sugar paste
Green sugar paste

1. Using the template, cut Paw's face from the flesh-coloured sugar paste and two cap pieces from the dark-brown sugar paste

2. Mix a little dark-silver lustre wi' a tiny amount of lemon juice tae form a metallic paint and carefully paint the features

3. Assemble the cap pieces and secure wi' a little food glue, then roll a small piece of dark-brown sugar paste and flatten onto the cap tae form a button

Texturise the cap with the scrunched tin foil

4. Roll two pieces of white sugar paste tae the shape of Paw's moustache using the template as a guide tae size and shape

Score the moustache pieces using the back of your knife

5. Assemble a' the prepared pieces on top of the cake

Roll a piece of flesh-coloured sugar paste for Paw's nose and attach tae moustache

Cut a strip of green sugar paste approximately 1.5" wide by 5" in length tae form the tie, and attach

Roll a piece of green sugar paste intae a ball and shape intae a knot for the tie. Attach this tae the cake

6. Score a checked pattern intae the tie using the back of your knife

7. Finished cake

171

Teddy bear cupcakes

The Bairn asked if I could make her some cupcakes for her teddy bears' picnic and she was fair beaming from ear tae ear when I gave her these cute wee teddy bear cupcakes. They're almost too bonny tae eat!

Small brush
Piping nozzle

12 cupcakes
Brown sugar paste
Food glue
Black sugar balls
Blue sugar paste
Pink sugar paste

1. Using the brown sugar paste, roll two balls, one slightly larger than the other. These will form the heid and body

Using the brown sugar paste, roll four equal-sized balls intae teardrop shapes for the arms and legs

Using the brown sugar paste, roll two smaller balls, one for the ears and another for the face. Make an indentation in one of the balls and cut intae two equal pieces: these will form the teddy's ears

Gently flatten the final ball of sugar paste tae form the teddy's face

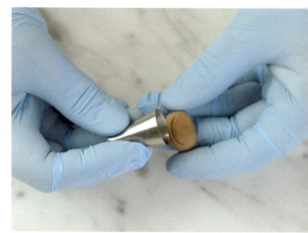

2. Using the wide end of the piping nozzle, mark a smile in the face piece

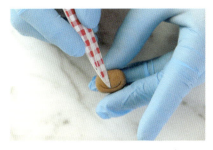

3. Score a crease in teddy's face using the blunt side of your knife

4. Using food glue, attach a' pieces together

5. Glue three small black sugar balls tae gie the teddy eyes and a nose

6. Add a blue bowtie for a boy

7. Add a pink hair bow for a girl

8. Final cake

Bagpipes cake

Granpaw cannae get enough o' the bagpipes, but after a' that hurling and skirling and showing aff his Highland dancin', he needs something tae get his energy back. That's why I made this special bagpipes cake.

14" round cake board
Jumbo straws
Pizza cutter
Knife
Small brush

10" round Madeira cake
1x basic buttercream recipe
Green sugar paste
Light-brown sugar paste
Red sugar paste
Black sugar paste
Food glue

1. Carve the cake intae the shape of the bag and cover wi' a layer of buttercream

2. Roll oot the green sugar paste and cover the prepared cake. Smooth over the shape and cut away any excess

176

3. Roll oot the light-brown sugar paste and prepare tae cut

4. Cut intae strips approximately ½" wide and 2" long

5. Roll oot the red sugar paste, cut ¼" strips and layer as in the photo

6. When ye are happy with the positioning, secure wi' a little food glue

7. Roll oot the black sugar paste and cover 3" x 3" and 1" x 5" straws using a little food glue

Roll oot a long sausage shape o' black sugar paste and wrap around the 3 shorter pieces

8. Assemble the prepared pieces as shown

Tae finish, roll oot a long piece of black sugar paste approximately 5" long and taper slightly at one end

Mark 6 holes using the end of your brush

9. Finished cake

177

Westie cupcakes

I made these as a wee treat for our picnic at the But 'n' Ben. A'body loves Westie dugs, so these pleased a' the family! It just takes a wee bit o' practice wi' your piping bag tae get the icing right, but they'll taste delicious no matter what.

Piping bag wi' small star nozzle

12 cupcakes
1x basic buttercream recipe
Marshmallow
Black sugar balls

1. Secure the marshmallow tae the cake wi' a little buttercream

2. Working from top tae bottom, pipe along the longer sides of the marshmallow and around the back

3. Pipe a swirl onto the front

4. Pipe a 'U' shape on each side tae form ears

5. Build up the face piping from the top tae bottom

6. Pop on the eyes using the black sugar balls

7. Finish using the black sugar balls
tae make the nose

Nessie cake

Now, when we went on a trip tae Loch Ness, the bairns were disappointed no' tae spot Nessie swimmin' aboot. So tae make up for it, I made this Nessie cake. The only thing was, the Bairn and the Twins made it disappear awfy fast, so once again Nessie was nowhere in sight!

Small brush
Tartan ribbon, long enough tae go around the cake
Knife

8" round cake, covered wi' sugar paste
White sugar paste
Light-blue sugar paste
Food glue
Light-grey sugar paste
Dark-green sugar paste
Light-brown sugar paste

1. Roughly mix the white and the light-blue sugar paste together tae form a two-toned water effect

2. Roll oot tae form an irregular circle and secure tae the cake wi' a little food glue

3. Shape the light-grey sugar paste intae a mound for the castle tae sit on and secure tae the edge of the water area

4. Make a small cube wi' the light-brown sugar paste and mark a few windows and turrets with your knife. Place on top of the mound

5. Roll oot the dark-green sugar paste tae form a sausage approximately 4'' long

6. Cut the green sausage shape intae four pieces each an inch in length, and bend two of these tae form Nessie's humps

Shape the remaining two green pieces intae Nessie's heid and tail

Attach a' remaining pieces onto the cake and secure wi' a little food glue, then tie the tartan ribbon around the bottom of the cake

7. Finished cake

181

Poinsettia cupcake wreath

Christmas is a time for something special, and mah poinsettia cupcake wreath makes a braw centrepiece – well, if the family can keep their hands aff it lang enough!

12" cake board
Piping bag with star nozzle
Small brush
Leaf plunge cutter

8 basic cupcakes
1x basic buttercream recipe
Red sugar paste
Green sugar paste
Food glue
Cream-coloured sugar balls

1. Using the leaf cutter, cut 3 red leaves and 6 green leaves for each cupcake: 24 red and 48 green in total

2. Using the food glue, assemble three-by-three leaf layers (2 x 3 green and 1 x 3 red)

3. Build up the three layers using a little food glue tae secure (red on top)

4. Brush a little food glue in the centre of the flower and randomly scatter wi' some of the sugar balls

5. Arrange the cupcakes in a circle and pipe each one with a little buttercream

6. Carefully place a flower on each cupcake

7. Makes a lovely Christmas gift

10

Bits
and
Bobs

Throughout the book I've referred tae various buttercreams and sauces that ye can use wi' a' kinds o' recipes, so here they are a' in one handy place! Why not mix and match and see what goes best wi' what. Or ye might even be tempted just tae whip up a batch o' buttercream a' on its own . . .

Basic buttercream

Basic buttercream can be used tae fill or top cakes and ye can adapt it wi' a' kinds o' flavourings. Experiment!

Electric mixer

150g unsalted butter, softened
300g icing sugar
A few drops of vanilla extract
10ml milk

1. Using an electric mixer, mix the butter, sugar and vanilla together

2. Add the milk and mix on full power for 5 minutes until smooth

Chocolate buttercream

This is mah basic buttercream but wi' one important addition – chocolate! Need I say more?

Electric mixer
Heatproof bowl
Saucepan

40g chocolate
100g unsalted butter, softened
300g icing sugar
40g cocoa powder
30ml milk

1. Melt the chocolate in a heatproof bowl over a saucepan of gently simmering water

2. Wi' an electric mixer, mix the butter, icing sugar and cocoa powder until smooth

3. Add the milk and melted chocolate, and beat on full power for 5 minutes

Chocolate ganache

Silky and smooth, chocolate ganache is a decadent addition tae any cake.

Heatproof glass bowl
Saucepan

500g dark chocolate, broken intae pieces
300ml double cream

1. Add the chocolate tae a heatproof glass bowl

2. Place the cream in a saucepan and heat over a medium heat until almost boiling

3. Pour the cream over the broken chocolate and stir until a' the chocolate is melted and the mixture is smooth

Tips

1. Pour over a cake tae gie a glossy finish

2. Whip tae gie a light mousse, which is perfect for piping

3. When allowed tae cool, it can be spread over a cake tae gie a firm coverage

Sugar paste

If ye don't want tae buy sugar paste and hae the time tae make it, this recipe will make aboot a kilo.

Heatproof bowl
Electric mixer

125ml glucose syrup
15ml glycerin
15g gelatin
15ml cold water (ye may need a little more)
900g icing sugar

1. Add the glycerin and glucose syrup tae a heatproof bowl, then add the gelatin and water and let it stand for a minute or two until it softens

2. Heat in a microwave for 30 seconds, then stir. Repeat until the liquid is clear and then allow tae cool. (Ye can heat in a bowl over a pan of hot water as an alternative tae the microwave)

3. Sieve the icing sugar intae a bowl and add the glucose mixture

4. Use your electric mixer, wi' a dough hook or similar, tae slowly mix. Add a little extra water if needed until ye hae a ball of the mixture

5. Dust your work surface wi' a little icing sugar and knead the ball until it's smooth

6. Add your food colouring – it needs tae be paste or gel food colouring

7. Tae store, wrap in cling film and a sealable plastic bag

Caramel sauce

Sweet and sticky, caramel sauce is the most delicious of them a'!

Heavy-based frying pan

250g caster sugar
60ml water
50g unsalted butter
140ml double cream

1. In a heavy-based frying pan, add sugar and water

2. Place over a medium heat and stir until a' the sugar dissolves

3. Turn up the heat and allow tae cook for a few minutes until it reaches a caramel colour

4. Remove the saucepan from the heat, add butter and cream, and beat until smooth

Tip

Can be eaten either hot or cold

Strawberry sauce

This is used as part of mah strawberry tart, but it's delicious on its own or drizzled over ice cream.

Heavy-bottomed saucepan
Food processor

125ml water
125g caster sugar
300g strawberries, hulled and halved

1. In a saucepan, add the water and sugar and bring tae the boil

2. Add the strawberries and leave tae cook for 2 tae 3 minutes

3. Allow tae cool and puree the mixture with a food processor

Tip

1. Can be stored in the fridge for up tae 2 days

2. Fill a freezer tray with the puree tae have some always on hand

Index

EAT, DRINK
& BE BRAW